RECLAIMED

RECLAIMED

RAY COOK

BALBOA.
PRESS

A DIVISION OF HAY HOUSE

Balboa Press books may be ordered through booksellers or by contacting:
Balboa Press
A Division of Hay House
1663 Liberty Drive
Bloomington, IN 47403
www.balboapress.com
1-(877) 407-4847

Because of the dynamic nature of the Internet, any web addresses or
links contained in this book may have changed since publication and
may no longer be valid. The views expressed in this work are solely those
of the author and do not necessarily reflect the views of the publisher,
and the publisher hereby disclaims any responsibility for them.

The author of this book does not dispense medical advice or prescribe the use
of any technique as a form of treatment for physical, emotional, or medical
problems without the advice of a physician, either directly or indirectly. The
intent of the author is only to offer information of a general nature to help you
in your quest for emotional and spiritual well-being. In the event you use any
of the information in this book for yourself, which is your constitutional right,
the author and the publisher assume no responsibility for your actions.

Any people depicted in stock imagery provided by Thinkstock are models,
and such images are being used for illustrative purposes only.
Certain stock imagery © Thinkstock.

Printed in the United States of America.

ISBN: 978-1-4525-8244-3 (sc)
ISBN: 978-1-4525-8246-7 (hc)
ISBN: 978-1-4525-8245-0 (e)

Library of Congress Control Number: 2013916653

Balboa Press rev. date: 9/20/2013

I dedicate *Reclaimed* to all of us actualizing our innate, divine worthiness and power; to my partner, Kirk, who's loved me through the process of loving myself; to my parents, who've always believed in me; and to universal grace and love.

CONTENTS

PREFACE

Regardless of supposed quality of life and exciting prospects for an auspicious future, I still felt empty inside and unhappy. Whenever I didn't busy myself as distraction, I was alone to feel my residual "less than" sentiments. I needed help and wanted to break my cycle of habituated behaviors of temporary, unfulfilling remedies.

I used to have stigma against psychotherapy—until I gave it a try. After marked self-improvement from my experience in Utah, I became an avid advocate. However, my first therapist in Boston was ice cold, and our mutual antipathy was visceral. Reluctantly thanking her for her time, I tactfully explained my discomfort and feeling of incompatibility. She confirmed. It's still hard to comprehend how her referral to Greg Lippolis, LICSW, came through such an awful experience. He was a godsend who got to the core of me and helped to identify and heal my root issues. I had buried them and ignored their insidious toxicity. Greg was who I needed to guide my navigation and transformation. His service was integral and invaluable to my healing, and I'm forever grateful.

Not long into our sessions, he asked if I would ever consider writing my stories, not only for my own benefit, but also for the help they could offer others if I shared them publicly. Initially, I didn't take him seriously. I was depressed and trying to understand my shortcomings and find purpose and meaning for my future.

Throughout school, I did not like writing and tried to avoid it at all costs. The thought of undertaking such an endeavor seemed daunting at best. For so long, I had discounted my stories as being insignificant, and I was reticent, afraid of disapproval and rejection.

Upon further encouragement and persuasion from Greg, I tearfully acquiesced. I trusted him and had faith in our work together. In January 2009, I brainstormed a list of possible anecdotes that I'd be willing to compose, adding and deleting throughout the developmental process. As the project progressed, I became cognizant that some of the stories were solely proofs of graphic smut scenes. Although I'm proud of how I was able to put them into words, I'm not proud of enabling my participation in them in the first place. The common denominators as I subjected myself to compromising circumstances were a state of mind conducive to such unbecoming behavior and flagrant disregard. Those stories were omitted, as I deemed them incongruous to my intended theme. I did not want to include salacious material for the sake of entertainment alone.

As a flight attendant, I took advantage of downtime during flights and on layovers to freehand my thoughts. The slower pace of pen to paper enabled me to deliberate over my composition. However, some of the heavy stories emotionally drained me, and the surfacing pain discouraged me from continuing, but I was already invested. I wanted to heal. After such stories, I had to take a break, sometimes for months, before I was ready to resume another anecdote. The upside, though, was that the elapsed time in between writings gave me emotional distance and objectivity.

The metamorphosis of *Reclaimed* was motivational, and the writing itself was profoundly cathartic and ultimately healing. Thank you, Greg, for planting the seed and nurturing its germination.

ACKNOWLEDGMENTS

I 'm grateful for my personal cheerleaders who've showed me their loving support, encouraged me to do what I had to do to be happy, and believed in me all along. Thank you Dad and Mom, thank you Kirk, and thank you to all my other "teachers" who've helped to facilitate my life lessons.

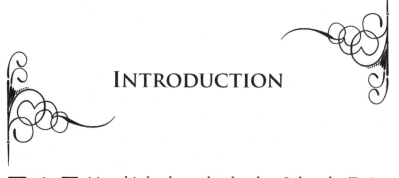

INTRODUCTION

Writing this book was harder than I thought. Trying to compose the tapes in my head stirred up a lot of buried emotions and left me wondering if I was really up to exposing my internal vulnerabilities. Not realizing the severe ramifications of unresolved issues, I had subconsciously postponed their antidote and subsequent healing by down-playing the repercussions of traumatic experiences and understating the arduous courage that they demanded. Internal validation has been a work in progress, and I'm grateful that I didn't let my fear sabotage this undertaking. Having let others' opinions of me, along with my own insecurities control me for so long, it was easy for me to hesitate about full disclosure. Despite sporadic qualms, I seriously considered my impetus to follow through. My conviction in the lessons had to be greater than the personal risk. I owe my survival to my higher power, optimism and gratitude.

These are my personal memoirs dealing with Mormonism, sexuality, coming-of-age, and my journey from lost to found. My stories may offend you, shock you, inspire you . . . My intent is to offer hope that regardless of your circumstances, life is manageable and happiness is a choice. These are my lessons learned.

SOUTHERN EXPOSURE

On a layover as a flight attendant, I went out on the town with a colleague. It was one of the few times when I wasn't the youngest, although that seems to be happening more frequently now. I like to socialize with older people, not to retain my status as the youngest, but because I feel more compatible with them, enjoy their maturity, and glean valuable lessons from their wisdom and experience. I hope that I keep us spontaneous, curious, and unjaded by life. I like to believe that we have somewhat of a symbiotic relationship, although I'll always feel indebted to their contributions to my personal development.

So I was telling my younger cohort how I seldom get carded at bars and confidently stated that turning thirty wasn't going to change that, but it was I, not him, who was carded. He had the biggest smirk of satisfaction. I reminded him that time stands still for no one, so he should enjoy boyish good looks while they lasted. It happened to be amateur strip night, and all the college boys were back in town. I observed all the attention focused on their youth: wrinkle-free faces, ripped bodies, smooth, flawless skin—and oh, their energy! All this was reminiscent of my former dancing days—flashbacks of the adoration, money, propositions . . .

I had just returned from Germany and didn't want my budding self-discovery to be oppressed back in Idaho. So I opted to move in with Peter and his boyfriend in Memphis. I quickly settled in with a restaurant job and applied to transfer colleges. My twenty-second birthday was not too long after I relocated, and I felt like going out. Peter and his boyfriend stayed home, so I went to the gay bar alone and luckily arrived (unbeknownst to me) before the strip show started. I watched and lusted after the two sexy men, both muscular and toned, with bulging packages. My mind was racing with hard-core fantasies of all the possibilities. After all, though I was still inexperienced, I was an always curious and apt pupil. At the end of their routines and working the crowd for tips, they approached me. I was surprised and confused. One of them introduced himself as the manager, and asked to speak with me back in their changing room. I was intrigued, but nervous. I had no clue what we were going to talk about, but I was hoping to be taken advantage of—just as I had played out in my mind.

Walking into their changing room, the manager complimented my looks and asked if I'd like to join them—as a dancer. That was quite a loaded question for me, having never even thought of such a thing. I had a serious body-image complex. I didn't believe that I had a body worth flaunting; I didn't feel that I ever had that "it" factor. Such a concept eluded me. I was so self-critical and -conscious. It was hard to think about anything but saying yes, though, as they both were stark naked by that point, changing. That night, after the thrill of the proposition subsided, the fear and anxiety set in. My obsessive-compulsive tendencies in regard to my body were amplified. I panicked and called the manager, trying to rescind my agreement to join. Let's face it—I lacked experience, but most critically, I lacked self-confidence. How could I possibly strut my stuff with such paralyzing insecurities?

Trying not to talk myself out of it, I held onto the manager's reassuring pep talks. He invited me over to coach me a little. We watched scenes from *Coyote Ugly*, and I was taking as many mental notes as my mind could absorb. He actually prepped me pretty well, which eased my anxiety. I practiced various moves and was thinking about which music to use, etc. My confidence was building when I thought of it like a performance. I was used to being in front of crowds; now it just demanded less costume. I don't remember the details, but my closing lesson found us fucking each other on his couch.

He recruited a good-looking boy my age who was pretty muscular. We both were novice and nervous about our debut. The drive from Memphis to Nashville was long as I lay across the backseat of the car, my stomach knotted in anxiety. The prepping in our changing room above the bar was surreal: the adrenaline, the dick needles and pumps, the fluffing. The music from below was thumping through the floor, the vibrations accentuating the churning of my insides. My nerves were intense. The other kid went out first. I heard his music cue, and as the crowd cheered him on, I started to dread my upcoming performance. He came back upstairs with a beaming smile, his face radiating the crowd's adoration and cash bulging out of his socks and thong, both serving as evidence of his triumph. The pressure was on. I had to deliver. I knew then that I had to rely on a unique niche, as I had neither the bulky muscles nor the bravado and swagger that exuded, "Look at me, I'm so sexy!" So I decided to incorporate my tumbling abilities—floor gymnastics—into my act. The first song was my performance song, "Sexual" by Amber. I intermittently stripped my random-themed costume as I flipped across the floor. The crowd loved it! Their cheers, claps, and whistles evaporated any remaining angst I was feeling. I had created my edge. The second song, "I Do Both Jay and Jane" by La Rissa, was my collection song as I graciously accepting their greenbacks in all denominations. They felt entitled to touch me, even places my mama told me not to, but I didn't resist nor rebuke. My craving made me a glutton for attention, and it was stronger than any discomfort of being objectified. I was being fed validation, albeit sexual and coupled with money, plus I felt wanted. The combination was a powerful drug, and I couldn't resist. I was desperate not only for money, but also for a sense of belonging . . . somewhere.

The three of us shared a hotel room that night. I woke up to the sight and sound of the manager fucking the (straight) kid. It was a bitter taste of jealousy. I quickly compartmentalized my mixed emotions.

I used to believe that if I didn't look like the smooth models in magazines, then I wasn't going to be wanted. So you can imagine my devastation when my body hair started growing. God, I hated the obsession to dehair myself. It nearly drove me crazy: shaving, Nair, clippers and trimmers, electrolysis—I tried everything to ameliorate the anxiety of my internalized imperfection. I believed that others with body hair (including myself) got a raw deal. I didn't understand the workings behind the scenes of photo shoots. I actually like body hair on other men, but I didn't think about others liking it on me. I could have saved myself a lot of grief by accepting my body hair and realizing its attractiveness. Peter would help me "manscape" before my strip shows, trimming my body hair with clippers (unbeknownst to his boyfriend). That was such a huge favor to me—I trusted him to relieve me from my stress over the pursuit of meticulous perfection. Plus, I enjoyed the pleasure of being touched all over, without expectation of any sexual reciprocity. Afterward, I would soak in a hot bath, listening to Enigma and drifting to sleep, entranced, until awakened by the tepid water becoming cold.

Late one night, after returning from my show at the bar, Peter and I began to masturbate (separately), watching porn in the living room. Although it was platonic, like buddies, his boyfriend woke up and walked in on us. Needless to say, he flew off the handle. In my immature mind, I hadn't done anything egregious, and it wasn't intimate from my point of view, but nevertheless, I could understand his rage. This situation manifested his fears and insecurities, which exposed his seething jealousy of my friendship and closeness with Peter.

The money came too easily, but I was mostly excited to see more of the country, booked for a three-city gig across the Midwest. I waited for the manager to pick me up—waited until I knew I was waiting in vain. I called him repeatedly, getting only his voice mail. I finally reached him and received the explanation that his boyfriend was jealous of me and didn't want him to be around me. I didn't even know he had a boyfriend, so how was I an issue? What about the other kid? Unless . . . the other kid was the (new) boyfriend? Either that or I upstaged their shows, and they didn't want me around, stealing their thunder? Maybe both scenarios? I had to figure out my next move and fast, because I had already quit my restaurant job. It didn't take long to decide what I was going to do. I was learning rapidly that if I was going to be taken care of, I'd have to do it myself. My faith in others kept diminishing with each disappointment and letdown—and abandonment.

With my bag already packed, and the weekend wide-open with no pending obligations, I decided to hit the road. I needed to anesthetize my looming panic about what would come next and how I'd survive, so I reverted to road-tripping as escapism. Driving alone, I felt free, adventurous, and excited—receptive to serendipitous gifts from the universe. I had to find my own gig. Brainstorming the geography within a reasonable radius of Memphis, the most viable attraction was New Orleans. I had never been there before, and its reputation gave me hope of employment for my newly discovered job skills. The seven-hour drive was exhilarating as I imagined all the possibilities and opportunities. Adventure was the antidote to my angst, and curiosity fueled my impulsive wanderlust. Interstate 55 was walled in by lush, green trees on either side. I have a propensity for speed, and as I was speeding, I laughed at myself, thinking about what I'd tell the cop why I was in such a hurry.

Somehow, my instincts brought me to the French Quarter. I changed my clothes to "apply" for a dancing job. As I walked,

I soon found out that I was near the gay end of Bourbon Street. I had nothing to lose, so I boldly asked to speak with the hiring managers of each gay bar I passed. It wasn't long before I came upon a corner bar that drew me in immediately with its open access to the streets. I was excited and nervous but mostly in awe: the patrons, the wooden bars acting as catwalks for the practically naked dancers who commanded attention, the music, the dance floor, the energy . . . Awe quickly became angst as I remembered my objective for being there. Did I really believe that *I* could be one of those dancers? They put my novice experience to shame, raising the bar much higher than I'd expected. I stood against the back wall, staring at their perfect bodies and observing their modi operandi. I was disappointed by their standoffish attitude. In my opinion, dancers are supposed to *dance*, not just expect cash deposits into their boots, as if sexiness deserved it on its own merit. I happened to be standing next to a handsome, fit, silver fox (typically my type). His name was Mike, and I told him my purpose for being there. He seemed amused and said he knew the manager. He told me to wait and left. I was curious . . . was this my lucky break? He returned with the manager, who led me through the staff area and up to his office. Without any sexual preconditions, I was hired on the spot to join those who I thought were out of my league up on the bar tops the following weekend.

DANCER FOR MONEY

Mike invited me to move in with him. Everything I owned fit neatly into Tupperware containers with snap-on lids and locking latches. I stacked them flush into the black Dodge Neon Sport that Peter bought me (another reason his boyfriend hated me). Mike's place was nice, in a peaceful, newly developed community on the West Bank outside of New Orleans—Marrero, to be exact. My brief two-month stay would consist of push-ups and running along the rural road through the adjacent hinterland during the week and dancing on Bourbon Street over the weekend. Despite the sticky heat and humidity, the remote solitude was a welcomed reprieve from the demands of my livelihood. Mike was falling for me, but I didn't have the balls to tell him that it wasn't reciprocal. I felt bad for leading him on, and I'm not proud to admit that I was self-absorbed, trying to figure out my next chapter.

As I walked toward the bar each night, I was drawn to the thumping crescendo of the music. Nearing the bar, my heart raced and my stomach churned with anxiety, knowing what was demanded of me . . . my expected exposure and vulnerability. My most memorable experience occurred not long after I entered the scene. I was writhing to the music, dancing euphorically, dripping sweat, entranced. Momentarily, I thought of how not long before, I was a Mormon missionary, proselytizing in Germany . . . and now I was gyrating around the bar in my skivvies, my socks stuffed with lust money. I had come far (in which direction is subjective). Ironically, I was more sincere and spiritually inclined at this stage than I was as a missionary. Tears welled as I looked up to keep them from draining down my face. What I felt was the same feeling that I was taught in the Mormon church to be the Holy Ghost (the Spirit). It was like God's stamp of approval that I was okay and didn't have to hate myself anymore. I had felt that before as a missionary, which was pivotal in my reconciliation between spirituality and self-integrity.

I had to change outfits as they became drenched in sweat. I was a dancer, and I actually danced, instead of just standing there like the other lame dancers who expected tips just for gracing the patrons with their presence and good looks. That attitude disgusted me—totally unsexy in my book. Besides not having the body confidence or personality to do so, I kept to what I felt was natural and most entertaining—dancing to have fun and crouching down to converse face-to-face with my audience. The locals told me I was their preferred dancer and admired my personality. That was worth more to me than the money. I knew that the other dancers had "other activities" for ancillary revenue, but I never thought that I'd be propositioned for such. I knew that I didn't want to do porn or prostitution. I had used my body before for easy money. Three separate times, a car had pulled up to me on the side of the road, each of the men offering me money in exchange for my company: one man wanted me to jerk off while he watched; another man wanted me to jerk him off; and in my most lucrative transaction, the man asked me to let him suck me off in exchange for paying my credit card bill.

The thrill of the moment was fun—the flattery, the lust, the risk, plus the fact that I needed the money. However, selling myself didn't leave me feeling proud. If I wanted to play, it was going to be on my own terms and of my own volition like at the bathhouse after work, but not out of desperation for money. The only time that I was hired to strip outside of the bar was at a private, coed party, and socializing with them actually turned out to be fun for me.

The weekends became crazier and the job less fun as I had to deal with the unbecoming behavior of inebriated and horny men. Some of them I labeled "losers"—those who drain your energy without replenishing it with anything edifying, who offer no substantial goodness and just use you to gratify their twisted agendas. Their aura and attitude emanated negative vibes. At least I learned from them what I don't want in my life. I was still too naïve, though, and oblivious to the dangers to which I subjected myself, such as walking alone to my car with a duffle bag full of cash. I'm lucky that nothing bad ever happened to me. Before leaving, the (former) club owner would offer me cocaine and invite me up into the attic to join the raunchy goings-on. Always curious, I was a voyeuristic witness upon occasion, but I wouldn't dabble in "party-and-play" until later in life.

I have an affinity for adventure (and risk), even if I sometimes have to force myself against my timid nature. I like to portray boldness until I feel bold. What a flash it was—that brief yet profound whirlwind that was my stint as a strip dancer. I'm glad that I kept a copy of *Eclipse: The Guide to Gay Nitelife in the Deep South* (now out of print). Ironically, my novice counterpart from Memphis and I are featured on the same page, representing opposing bars in New Orleans (6, no. 20 [2001]: 22). Initially, I hoarded copies to distribute and show off, but now I keep only one copy for myself, for the sake of reference, as proof. I don't know if I could go back and do it all again. Actually, no, I do know that I could not—no more preventing rolled bills from being inserted into my ass, no more lying on the bar with only a bouquet of balloons covering my package while the bartender sucked shots out of my naval, no more covering my full monty with just a bar towel as I paraded back and forth on the bar. However, I fondly reminisce just dancing (with underwear) and conversing—not debasing my character.

The immersion into exposing my body was the catalyst that changed my negative body image and enabled me to accept myself. One might think that one dances out of ego just for money, but ultimately, I needed to dance to develop self-appreciation, -confidence, and -approval. The adoration I received, even from lecherous trolls, I soaked up like a sponge. I didn't see myself desirable. The sexual attention was a paradox of hedonism and self-help. I was hungry to forge my own story, to escape from my life that I considered blasé. I wanted to create and naturalize copious experiences as a world citizen. It all strengthened my humanity and empathy. It was a fun and exciting personal growth spurt with mixed emotions.

I remember proudly informing my family of my new location and job. I knew that I wasn't degrading myself and that I was holding my ground amidst such environs, but I didn't consider how my family might interpret my excitement as boastful degradation from their values. Although I was getting attention from strangers, I longed for the attention from my family, which I didn't feel that I was getting. Perhaps I used this disclosure for shock value to get their attention, hoping for their validation and support, but I was just fooling myself. I should've known better than to share too much, but I wanted so desperately for them to know that I was okay and not on the decline. Regardless, being honest about it released me from future feelings of guilt or shame that accompany secrecy. Of course, it didn't sit well with my conservative family, and their silence grew louder. At least when they preached down to me, it was a form of attention, albeit a condescending one. However, this time, I interpreted their lack of acknowledgment as indifference to my life. If anything, by pushing their buttons, intentionally or not, I had tainted our relationships and driven them further away, making it harder for them to accept me. I was on a quest to redefine my individuality, even if it meant breaking protocol and defying adherence to expectations, especially from a religious platform. Exploring novel life experiences contributed to my self-confidence, and acting in accordance with my authentic self improved my self-esteem.

MOTORBIKE

Growing up, I rode motorbikes with my dad and brothers. I loved the freedom and fun it offered me in our rural neighborhood. I was told not to ride alone, especially on the highway. One day, after a church activity, a neighbor boy asked if I would give him a ride home. We lived on the same road, but I knew that I'd have to cross the highway. I wanted to impress him because he was one of the "cool" kids. I dropped him off and headed home. At the highway intersection, I remember looking both ways, and even twice to the right because it was a bright day. I crossed, and saw the car just before it hit me. My Sunday school teacher crashed into me at sixty-five miles per hour. Everything was in slow motion. I remember thinking to myself, *Oh well,* and intuition prompted me to rise up on the foot pegs.

I don't remember any pain during the immediate aftermath, but I looked down at my mangled body in the gutter (my motorbike flung around a telephone pole). I instinctively redirected myself toward the clouds. I felt no bodily restrictions nor limitations of gravity. I could fly by thought, but ascent into the ineffable sublime was frustratingly blocked. Disappointingly, I was rudely awakened two days later to a confusing confinement in a hospital—and the news that I was lucky—struck any lower, my pelvis and spine would've been crushed by the car's bumper, impact any further up or to the left, my skull would've been crushed by the car's windshield frame. Gravel was still stuck in my scalp, my leg was in contraction and elevated by a pulley in front of me. I had a metal rod inserted down my right femur (in conjunction with the bone marrow), and my body cast wrapped around my waist, continuing down past my knee.

I didn't want to be back. My soul knew where home was, but my time down here was not up yet.

MEMBER DAMAGE

At an early age, I was treated as an outcast by most of my peers because of my darker skin, as well as for being smart. The ostracism became acute when I skipped from second grade into third grade. I was so bored during school, always finishing my work early and doing something else during class. I didn't think it was fair that my teacher would assign me extra work, like punishment for excelling. My dad did some research and asked if I wanted to take a placement test for an opportunity to skip ahead a grade. I was ecstatic. My third grade teacher didn't make me feel welcome in his class and did nothing to intervene with my new classmates relentlessly belittling and teasing me. I was often sent to the principal's office because I wouldn't do extra work without explanation, and I questioned both their authority. I felt that my teacher and principal were in cahoots against me. I never felt that they were on my side—no encouragement, no praise, all discipline. I'm pretty sure that's when I began to defy and resent authority figures.

Looking back on my youth, I see that internalized guilt and shame held me hostage. I felt that I lost my innocence when I started masturbating—that's when my demons intensified. I lived an innocent childhood, but as puberty set in, sexual hormones made me feel sinful. Sex was taboo, which made it seem shameful. I lost joy in simple things because I obsessed about my sinful thoughts condemning me for eternity. I was a perfectionist, so how could I be perfect, thinking these thoughts—amplified by my hormonal body sabotaging me?! Being gay was condemning enough in Mormonism, especially with the religion's injurious, judgmental literature explicitly vilifying homosexuality as a heinous sin with grave consequences and masturbation (even in marriage) as sinful. For the first time in my life, I contemplated suicide after reading (and believing) such pernicious bigotry and ignorant dogma. My glow was snuffed out and my self-image plummeted. I desperately wanted to belong to my family and church, but didn't know how to do so without betraying myself.

Every time I got an erection, I hated my body for setting me up for an abysmal hell. I would wrap my dick in duct tape day and night. It hurt too much, so I accidentally discovered that by pressing down hard enough, it would snap/pop under pressure and my erection would subside. Only later did I find out while visiting a urologist (unbeknownst to my parents) that I had caused permanent damage, building up scar tissue on the side of the shaft. Without surgery, I'd forever have a slight bend instead of a straight erection. Was I the only one with a body inferiority complex? I wanted to look like the toned athletes at school, smooth like the models in magazines. I could change and control those temporary adjustments, but what about my dick? Even if my external looks got the sexual attention I desired, would my dick be a deal-breaker? Fear of rejection altered how I felt about myself. I chose to shell up, instead of being confident. My choices and behaviors reflected my cowardice thoughts. My body inferiority complex resulted in risk-aversion, and the onset of my obsessive-compulsive tendencies to perfect myself physically, if I couldn't "cleanse" my repressed homosexual identity. I despised the Mormon church even more for not only preaching my damnation, but also instilling in me the belief that my natural body functions were sinful. I blamed the Mormon church for years to come, for causing physical damage on top of tearing me apart psychologically.

I searched the public library references for gay bars in San Francisco. Then, at home, I would muster up enough courage to dial their numbers, just to listen to another gay voice. I would ask some inane questions just to keep whoever answered on the line, imagining myself taking part in the background noise of the other men, but would feel deflated when the brief conversation was over. I'm sure he knew I was a shaking, curious minor by my voice and hesitancy. Afterward, I would fantasize about what it might be like there. I envisioned the profligate stories I had previously read in the limited references of "gay/homosexuality" in the library. I would ensconce myself in a chair near that aisle, anticipating others besides myself to browse. I was so hungry! I wanted a role model to guide me through this unsupported, taboo identity.

MY CRAZIES

I got into my hotel room well after midnight, but my inconsistent sleep schedule as a flight attendant had me wired. So I poured myself a tumbler of wine ("Hello, my name is Billy Ray, and I'm . . . dealing!" was my possible introduction at a hypothetical AA meeting). I'm naturally optimistic about everything, so I'm surprised when painful emotions surface. My whole life I've hidden my obsessive-compulsive tendencies, because even I know they're irrational, and I ridicule myself in the process. Science confirms that obsessive-compulsive tendencies are not mental, but chemical. I've struggled to keep it at bay, and thankfully, I've managed without medication—although sometimes I tire of forcing myself to alter the chemistry and want to give in to a pill . . . or seven! I've heard and read that physically forcing oneself not to follow through with compulsions actually alters chemicals affecting those behaviors in the brain, as seen in brain scans. However, even before I was aware of that, I experienced it to be true.

The memories came flooding back and I was crying, feeling sorry for myself. I was anxious and uncomfortable, revisiting those awful memories—the fucking torment! I wasted so much time and energy trying to perfect and control every aspect of my life. I wanted to enjoy a carefree day like anyone else, but I was wracked with internal prison guards disciplining me: to align objects flush or with exact spatial equity, to throw away and redo reports because the pencil lead wrote darker as it dulled, to continue to obsess about numbers/letters/patterns and how they looked/sounded/flowed, to pick at the cushions on my crutches because they weren't smooth enough or symmetrical (resulting in having to buy new pads altogether because I picked them apart to nothing), to break the headlights dial in the car to physically "feel" the off-position, and to repeat it all. Even if I forced myself out of scratching the itch of one nagging obsession, another would surface. I relate these ticks to a scratch in a record, repeating its insanity until the needle is forced out of the groove. I let these obsessive thoughts compel me to repeat ritualistic absurdities, which robbed me of enjoying the present moment.

The worst was the physical torture of tweezing my eyebrows off—thrice—and the resulting amplified self-consciousness and embarrassment. Thank God for eyebrow pencil! My guard would be down when I'm tired, and I would tell myself to go to bed, that I wouldn't feel the anxiety in the morning. I couldn't sleep, though, imagining the catastrophic spiral of events that could occur: people who might criticize me, what they might say, how it would make me feel. What would they think? Oh, how my cumbersome rituals exacerbated my ruthless self-critic. I would stand in front of the mirror, seeking out any flaw or imperfection in the pattern or length of my eyebrows. I'd tweeze the obvious excess, but then, when I rationally knew that I was finished, my irrational chemicals would compel me to tweeze more. My body would start to ache, maneuvering around the counter and sink, contorting positions to create the best lighting and, by God, to tweeze the last follicle! All the while, I'd tell myself to *Stop, stop, stop,* that it was just the obsessive-compulsive tendencies getting the best of me. It was already way too out of control. Tweezing temporarily relieved my anxiety, but perpetuated the cycle. I'd plead with myself to stop, to save the little I had left, telling myself that would be better than having them completely gone. I hoped to leave at least something to serve as a semblance of a base to make the new growth not look so drastic.

I'd plead again, this time with God, bargaining to let me off the hook—just one more hair, then I'd be satiated, and my anxiety would be tamed. But hell no—if I had already fucked them up, then I was going to really fuck them up! I was tired to begin with, but by the time I was done, I was exhausted and humiliated. I didn't want to have any obligations or responsibilities for the next couple weeks so that I could just stay home and not be seen in public.

Perhaps part of my all-or-nothing behavior stems from the black-or-white Mormon teachings that were drilled into me. How can you expect intrusive codes of conduct and thinking not to influence your psyche? Why were my eyebrows so important, and not something else? I don't know. I knew (from compliments) that my eyes and smile drew others to me, which is why I obsessed about them. Thinking back, I probably punished myself subconsciously for perceived spiritual shortcomings about being gay and having sex, by tweezing too much, too far—my anxiety was physically manifesting itself. Why couldn't I have been gentle with myself? Why did I feel so inadequate?

I would cry, not knowing how to stop, and knew that I needed help. I sought a high school counselor, and what a godsend she was. She didn't think I was crazy, nor did she judge me like I judged myself. I enrolled in her self-esteem class my junior year. It was serendipitous and exactly what I needed. The class was small, divided into groups around individual tables. We each had a manual with exercises (individual/group), positive affirmations, goal-setting, self-evaluation, etc. She also led us in class meditation at the end, to solidify our work together and to accept our state of being. She sincerely cared and encouraged me to accept my imperfections. She taught me how to self-talk out of self-sabotaging spirals and to discredit life-disturbing perfectionism. (How could the varsity cheerleading queen be sitting next to me . . . in *that* class? How did we become friends, carpooling to gymnastics? Why did she choose *me* to be our senior year mascot?) I wasn't any sort of popular throughout school. I didn't have the self-image whatsoever, so I escaped into tumbling, school, and church. I was a cute kid (and humble), but in my teens, my harrowing, self-defeating, and intrusive self-critic set in. I didn't like my wonkish looks . . . I didn't like myself in general. I felt so awkward, and my school photos reflect that unease. I was so socially inept and timid, projecting my insecurities as I walked with my head down between slumped shoulders.

Self-talk and forcing myself not to give in to the compulsions is agonizing work, but it helps. The urge diminishes when I force myself not to act out, even though it feels like mental anguish. I have to keep myself in check, always. It's never easy. I remember going to see a counselor in junior college, and after he listened to my coping strategies, he had nothing more to add. I have to be aware of my state of being. For the most part, I have it under control. The only area in which habitual rituals still carry over is my personal grooming. I still challenge myself now and then to break the automatic, symmetric counting and application of soap and/or deodorant, but I surrender to the fact that at least it's beneficial. I have, however, through the same process of self-challenge, been able to break away from other grooming rituals: hair, clothes, etc. I'm not controlled by it anymore. My obsession has transferred to deleting clutter, whether it be tangible or informational or letting go of mental (co)dependency on people. I've become a minimalist, junking items after periods of only occupying space (unless it's sentimental)—this also applies to stored digital information, kept for the sake of "just in case," as well as contact information I hardly use, especially non-reciprocal contacts. It's my way of preventing relapse into codependency. Although deleting seems extreme sometimes, so was hoarding and clinging onto insufficient substitutes for love. Deleting sure beats where I used to be—needing anyone and everyone to fill my void, regardless the costs.

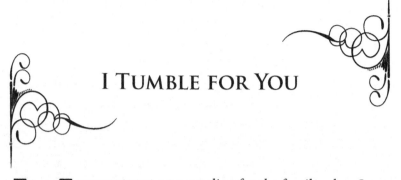

I TUMBLE FOR YOU

My parents got a trampoline for the family when I was five. I pretty much took it over, spending hours on it every day. The exhilaration, feeling my body fly through the air was like a drug. My tricks were self-taught, and I longed to execute them on the ground. My dad's poor head was whacked pretty hard when he spotted me doing a back handspring. I had set couch cushions, pillows, and blankets—anything soft I could find—onto the ground to cushion my fall. One time, I tried a back flip off our mini exercise trampoline. I flipped straight upside down and landed directly on my head on the carpeted cement floor. That was scary, and I was lucky not to have been hurt, as there were no cushions.

I loved watching the cheer and dance competitions on TV and dreamed of doing that someday. I also dreamed of being in the Olympics, but it didn't seem plausible, given where I lived and the cost of training. I knew that our local Mormon junior college had a cheerleading team, so I wanted to be a part of it. My dad was generous to fund my tumbling training, public and private. He witnessed the joy I had showing off my capabilities, and I thank him for supporting me, both financially and through his willingness to cheer me on. He made me feel significant. I joined the tumbling team in junior high and participated in our high school's coed drill team. I was a tumbling fool. I loved it! It was my escape, my passion.

My sheltered childhood in bucolic Idaho was quite conducive to an expected Mormon upbringing, offering few vices if even accessible. My exemplary behavior as a straight-A student and especially as a model Mormon boy was a cover-up for my internal dilemma: the tug-of-war between conformity and authenticity. Tumbling was my escape and avoidance, the natural high I depended on to sustain me through the constant, intensifying barrage of negative inner, religious, and cultural messages of inadequacy. The feeling of body awareness as I flipped through the air, the physics of motion, and the contact of my hands and feet with the floor were a self-approving rush. I knew that it looked awesome, because it felt awesome, and I needed to fill up my reservoir of liking myself to last me until the next training.

I couldn't bear to think about the imminent day of reconciling my truth, so I perpetuated a double life in order to deny my fear. Besides putting on appearances, I overcompensated for my perceived liability of being gay by excelling in academics, tumbling . . . and self-righteousness.

Late one night, the owner of the gymnastics gym invited me over to spend the night. He was in his forties and was an effectively stern figure at the gym. Along with training there, I also coached younger classes, and I was intimidated by him as a boss. However, I fantasized about being with him sexually, though I never thought he'd give me the time of day. So you can imagine my surprise and delight at his offer. *Me? Really?!* He offered me my first-ever alcoholic drink. We sat in his living room as he listened to me tearfully dump all of my pent-up guilt and fears onto him, crying about my predicament well into the early morning. Lying next to each other in bed, he pulled me in close to him, him lying on his back and me on my side—my leg straddling his, my arm across his stomach, and my head on his torso, the side of my face nestled on his hairy chest. I felt safe, comforted, yet disappointed that he didn't take advantage of me sexually. Maybe he didn't want to go there, realizing my mental torture with everything.

Maybe my complicated situation was too much with which to get involved. Whatever the reason, I've never forgotten. The next morning, he made us breakfast, showed me around his garden, and introduced me to his neighbor, who happened to be outside as well. That meant a lot to me, that he didn't act ashamed or treat me like I was some furtive mistake.

I was beside myself when I made it onto the collegiate cheerleading team. Better yet, that year would be the first for the team to qualify to compete at Nationals—the very televised event that I had watched and dreamed about. I was flying, literally, as the main tumbler on the Spirit Team. My coach emphasized her expectations of my performance, and I reveled in the feeling of being wanted, needed. We were going to compete at Nationals '97, and I was stoked! I was an honor student, heading into finals week. I was floored and unprepared for what was about to ensue.

MICKEY

I was driving to Salt Lake City every weekend (four hours each way) to be around other gay people. I had upgraded my teenage routine of driving to Pocatello to go to the adult bookstore, where I'd hopefully be cruised by other men. I was too shy at the time to initiate, as I was only sixteen, but I wasn't carded at the door. A man in his mid-thirties stared me down in one of the aisles and nodded his head for me to follow him out the door. He invited me back to his house. I was excited and nervous as I followed him in my car, wondering how my first adult sexual experience would unfold. He had an extensive porn collection in his basement . . . boxes and boxes. I would end up staying there a couple of times in the future, not remembering which lie I told my parents for them not to become suspicious of where I was or what I was doing. I was pretty independent (and a good kid), so I was allowed a lot of unsupervised freedom and leeway to come and go. As a natural people-pleaser, good behavior and curious defiance was a rich dichotomy. It was a win-win: following the "rules" pleased others, granting me privilege of which I exploited to get away with whatever I could. As far as discipline went, I always made it to where I needed to be, was a straight-A student, and stayed out of trouble, so I'm sure my parents didn't suspect anything. The man wanted me to fuck him, but I was naïve and inexperienced, so he rode my dick as I lay on my back. I was enthralled—not only was I having sex, but I was wanted as well.

Porn runs to Pocatello stopped when my dad caught me watching one at home, my hand down my pants. That was humiliating! He called my bishop immediately for a confessional interview.

I hated myself in general at that time. Many of my early experiences with men were as a minor, but I was in full consent. I usually had to talk them into being with me or just flat out lie about my age in order to be with them. I've always had a strong proclivity toward older men, finding something about age and maturity super sexy.

On my first trip to Salt Lake, I stopped at an adult bookstore to find out where the gay bars were. I found one but was nervous as hell. I hatched a plan: I would ask to use their phone book to find information about the university cheerleading program. It was still daytime, so I didn't even think about the possibility of the bar not being open (I'd never been to a bar before). Luckily, the staff was already preparing for later, and let me in. No patrons were there, but I didn't want to leave this "secret society" venue to which I had been granted access. I was feeling sheepish, knowing that my time at the phone booth was up, so I walked as cool as my false confidence would allow toward the door. I made it under the radar—sad to depart, but eager to return to the comfort zone of my car as soon as I could. I was not comfortable in my own skin. I almost made it to my car when I heard someone call out after me. My heart froze and then pounded. What now?! I hadn't prepared for this scenario in my head. The man motioned me back in. He was gorgeous. His name was Mickey. We sat by the front bar, the emptiness accentuating the spacious dance area. Why would someone go out of his way to talk with me? My internal dialogue was repeating, "It's okay. You're from No-town, Idaho. No one will know." I had conditioned myself to lie like a professional. I had to, for my perceived survival as a closeted Mormon depended on it. If I only knew then how hard it would be to untangle my web! I was so accustomed to deception that I was proud and ashamed at the same time. Little did I know that my chameleon ease would leave such a wake of hurt feelings, and enable me to continue self-destructive behaviors. No healing or coming into my own could ever start without first unraveling the wool I had pulled over my eyes. I was lost, unhappy, searching for my real identity . . . and afraid that the truth would invalidate me indelibly.

Without realizing it, my soul yearned for authenticity. Mickey asked, "So . . . where ya from?" I hesitated nervously, then answered honestly. I was relieved to tell him where I was from—that is, until he replied, "Oh really?! I'm from the next town over." My posture immediately sunk as I trembled inside, "Oh shit!" My eyes popped out of their sockets and my jaw was in my lap. He told me that he used to be a cop back home, and after exchanging some names, he claimed to know my sister-in-law (frequently pulling her over to flirt with her). I felt both excited and like I was going to throw up. I wanted to take my disclosure back, and he must have sensed my panic, because he didn't hesitate to reassure me of his confidentiality. Mickey became my first gay confidant and friend. He was a practical role model who didn't take advantage of me—and believe me, I wanted him to. I slept at his place one night after the bar closed. He was dating a guy at the time, so I slept on the couch, but I fantasized about him coming down sometime during the night to cuddle with me. I slept over a couple more times throughout the years, but he never made any moves. It was frustrating. I thought that I was somehow inadequate. How contradictory that I internally believed that I wasn't worthy, yet wondered *Why not me?* when it came to not being picked up. My internal beliefs were manifesting physically. Mickey was the bar manager, and his boyfriend was a bartender there. I despised the boyfriend for not really appearing to be that into him, and I viewed him as taking my spot. I guess Mickey was my first crush.

I felt like such a novice, so unsociable and shy in general, especially at the club. I envied those who held their heads high, their confidence threatening my existence. I would sit at the end of the bar, trying to be inconspicuous, too afraid to smile or make eye contact. Heaven forbid I speak to anyone! I was desperate for attention, though. I felt withered. After several comments to me during different visits that I should not look so serious and should smile more, I forced myself to baby-step toward sociability. It was terrifying. It took all the courage I could muster. However, the positive reinforcement would become my Pandora's box. (Attention?—Hi, my name is Billy Ray, and I'm an addict!)

Oh God, the learning curve was awkward! I still laugh at myself when I'm at a club and I remember myself clogging on top of the dance boxes in the middle of the floor. Yes, clogging—and doing the "Roger Rabbit" and "running man" dance moves. I can imagine the mockery and ridicule behind my back, for sure. I was oblivious and scared, but I wasn't going to just stand in the corner anymore like a wallflower. Mickey said if I was going to be there weekends anyway, he could use me as a doorman. Why not get paid for meeting citizens of my newfound mesmerizing world? I started then and there. One of the security men was a beefy, blond brute. Best of all, he liked me. It didn't take long for us to become an item, and it was the first time that I had genuine romantic feelings for another man. I was still a teen and he was in his thirties, but it just felt right. I've learned that for me, age doesn't define compatibility in a relationship. The best relationships I've had have been with men twenty-plus years my senior.

JOSH

I always felt a rush driving the freeway into the liberating city of Salt Lake. The thumping beats, strobe lights, sexy men, my clandestine affair—all the while attending a Mormon junior college, supposedly adhering to a mandated honor code of chastity and holiness. Practically from infancy, the Mormon dogma is indoctrinated into one's psyche, and weekly brainwashing reinforces its powerful grip. Corrosive guilt and shame become ingrained, knowing perfection is both impossible and expected, especially for image's sake. This implanted trip wire set off my conditioned compulsion to auto-correct. I felt an intensifying uneasiness as Nationals '97 approached. This event was to be the highlight for which I had trained so hard, my dream-come-true. However, I didn't want my lingering feelings of guilt to dilute the exhilaration, so I arranged a meeting with my college bishop to confess my "dating sins" with a guy in Salt Lake, because I didn't want a nagging conscience. Sexually, I hadn't gone far with that beefy, blond brute. My college bishop asked, "Have you been sexually active?" To which I denied, "Not really—just making out and "heavy petting" (the Mormon colloquialism for frottage). Sexual terminology was avoided as taboo and dirty, but if it were necessary for such confessions, such use carried shameful innuendo—extremely embarrassing at best.

He thanked me for my candor, and reassured me that I did the honorable thing. I felt relieved to "be in the clear"—so I thought, until I was summoned to meet with him again. He said, "I had no choice but to counsel with the Dean of Students . . ." My stomach knotted and all sound became white noise—even though I could still comprehend him. He continued, "I'm sorry that life isn't fair. My daughter can't do ballet anymore because of her tendonitis." I was infuriated. "What the hell did that have to do with anything?!" I seethed to myself with clenched teeth. He betrayed my confidence by reporting me to the Dean, and I was forced to either withdraw from school (without taking finals) or get expelled altogether.

I was crushed. I sank into a deep depression, and it terrified my parents to witness my glow and levity snuffed out (again). My hopes and excitement for life in general were dashed. There was no option other than telling my parents the truth. I wasn't ready to come out, nor had I dreamed of coming out in the future, but in retrospect, this incident redeemed my life from a (miserable) path that was already laid out and expected. If I had ever married a woman, it would have been invalid despite good intentions, premised upon complete fraud. The damage to myself and others (my future family) might have been irreparable.

Meanwhile, my roommate was boasting of his conquest of a girl—their "heavy petting" on campus grounds. Shortly thereafter, though, the girl confessed her guilt, and he was also summoned to meet with the same college bishop for questioning/confession. Instead of owning his part, he was angry at being turned in. His pride was hurt, and he cursed her—blaming her for his unknown consequences. I was still shell-shocked and silent about my own predicament. My roommate had no clue, so I didn't dare scare him by sharing my fateful sentence. He became paranoid, and I empathized with his state of limbo. I kept quiet—not to freak him out.

Insult was added to the injury of my punishment when my roommate only got one-month probation—then went on his mission (became a missionary), a rarefied privilege reserved only for those deemed worthy. I was learning firsthand of the hypocrisy and injustice of fallible men dictating their own agendas in the name of God and under the disguise of religion. Sadly, I broke off my relationship with the beefy, blond brute, because I was unable to deal with the blow. I wasn't mature enough yet to disassociate him from my fallout. I went online to see if anyone wanted to ride with me to Salt Lake (to split the cost of gas) for the weekend. I was lonely. A man named Josh replied. I stopped at his house in Pocatello to pick him up, and I was shocked to find out he was from the adjoining town to mine, closer even than was Mickey. He also knew my sister-in-law, the same one that Mickey knew. Why were these people coming into my life, so close to home? Later, I would acknowledge that something greater than myself had always provided good people in my life. Josh consoled me, taught me, encouraged me, and loved me. I give him significant credit for being a true friend, confidant, and source of support when I desperately needed it. I was so malleable, and I'm grateful to have been influenced by a kind, loving soul with my personal best interests in mind, even though it meant his own suffering. I was unavailable in many ways, and the hope of us becoming a long-term couple wasn't realistic, considering my journey ahead. Again, I was still a teen, and he was almost thirty. We both were young, and boy did I have a lot to learn!

I Tumble for You Again

I wanted to move on with my life, which meant getting out of Idaho, so I enrolled in travel school—and excelled. I've always loved traveling, so I figured that this would give me an insider's edge and get me out into the wonderful, wild world. I also love geography, so travel school was not only relatively easy, but fun! I learned world geography: its cultures, selling points, sights, activities, accommodations, etc. Along with the "fun stuff," came the not-so-fun (for me) technical industry systems. That was off-set by learning how to deal with clients/customers (a beneficial precursor to my unbeknownst future career). A classmate and I got recruited by Continental Airlines for their experimental class of International Reservations Agents—bypassing domestic training/reservations altogether. We moved to Salt Lake and became roommates. We both were from small towns in Idaho— eager for bigger and better—our independent and significant lives elsewhere. We enjoyed being silly and goofing off together, and would often find ourselves laughing hysterically. I slept on the couch, so I was delighted when she invited me to sleep with her in her big bed. ("Um, hello Ray!") I was clueless of her falling in love with me, until it became palpably uncomfortable—by the way she started cuddling me and by her progressively possessive control she exerted over my longing to become naturalized into the gay community. I felt my new freedom becoming stifled, so I found a shared apartment with two other gay guys.

When one of the guys fell in lust with me (and it wasn't mutual), I associated that unease with my previous experience. I started my pattern of running away from discomfort, rather than dealing with it. I got a call from my collegiate cheerleading coach, asking me to come back to tumble for the team for the upcoming school year. Nationals '98 was now a tangible expectation, unlike the surprise qualification in '97. I knew I had to play the Mormon game right this time, so instead of my former college-ward bishop, I contacted my home-ward bishop (whom I respect and consider a friend) to begin the process of matriculation. This meant jumping through the hoops of scrutiny: interviews, recommendations, contrite repentance, and my resolve to lie, lie, lie. Through trial and error, playing their game by their rules had sabotaged me. So this time, I was going to play by my own rules, giving them what they wanted to see and hear. I had one goal in mind, and I wasn't going to allow myself to be robbed again of the opportunity to compete.

I kept under the radar throughout the year, committed to my studies and cheer practice. Any "extra-curricular escapades" into the gay subculture were covert. No more guilt trips to the bishop! Only a select number of tumblers and stunters were chosen from our team to compete. Wow—how my ego inflated when our coach referred to me as the "head tumbler." I was literally flying—on cloud nine.

The convening of all competing teams at Disney World in Orlando was surreal. Our uniform was our identity and pride, and the warm-up practices were high-octane. Rotating teams on the practice mats gave each other competitive looks and attitude—intimidating enough to discourage even the cockiest among us. The night before competition was restless—excitement and nerves dominated sleep. Our team huddled backstage, awaiting our turn in anticipation as the music and cheers of the team before us haunted me. We said a team prayer, and during our pep-talk from our coach, I started silently crying—tears flowing down as

I was overcome with the reality of that moment and the pressure to execute our performance. It was really happening—and I was a part of it! Our coach looked at me and assertively affirmed, "You got this!"

As we got into position, the silence accentuated the tension. The adrenaline was intense, and as the music cued, I flipped across the floor with our opening tumbling pass. I was on fire, and my body felt in sync with the floor—the mechanics like a machine. As brief as our routine was, my tumbling felt spiritual and I was edified by the experience.

Nationals '98 was such a rush! The means to the end were well worth it.

CALLED TO SERVE

My parents had some Mormon missionaries over for dinner one night. I wanted my parents to revere me the way they revered missionaries. I was curious where I'd be "called to serve" (proselytize), regardless my lack of intention to go. One must fill out paperwork and go through interviews in order to be deemed worthy and qualified (along with other prerequisites) to serve as a missionary. The powers that be then receive revelation from God as to where each individual is "called" to serve most effectively. Traditionally, worthy boys at the age of nineteen (and worthy girls at the age of twenty-one, if not yet married) are expected to go away for two years/(one-and-a-half years respectively) to preach the gospel. Now, the age has been reduced to eighteen (not to interrupt college later)—my assumption is that the church doesn't want to lose missionaries to "the world." There's a missionary handbook of rules—the "white Bible" which lists expansive and inclusive restrictions in order to ultimately "leave behind all other personal affairs" such as: no family contact except for handwritten letters (now, email) and only two phone calls per year (Mothers' Day and Christmas), no contact with friends, and no media whatsoever—including: TV, film, radio, music, magazines, books, newspapers, etc. not authorized for missionaries (which is stricter than "church approved"). Of course, there's no separation from one's companion—like an attached prison guard. I told myself that I'd only consider going if it were somewhere German-speaking. I started developing a passion for German in high school, solidified by a one-month exchange program to Leipzig, Germany.

I felt that the Mormon faith was not true for me, so I schemed a plan to exploit the system. I conspired with my bishops (home and college) to keep my paperwork secret from my parents in order to surprise them. They had no more expectation of me to be a missionary. I didn't want to toy with my family's emotions, so I waited to decline in secret, without having to expose it. I significantly falsified my application, claiming German fluency and residence abroad. Even though a mission would be an exit out of Idaho, it still came with a high cost of expectations and work—a sacrifice I'd only make to immerse myself in Germany.

I had my mission call sent to Josh's place in Salt Lake. The anticipation, curiosity and fear of an impending decision was an emotional roller-coaster. The excitement about the idea of potentially going "somewhere" thrilled me. However, I didn't really want to actually commit myself to the role and requirements of a missionary. On a previous trip to Salt Lake, I met Josh's friend, Ed. We had an immediate attraction toward each other, and we started dating long-distance. Josh and Ed were both returned-missionaries, so I wanted them present to witness the suspenseful moment when I opened my letter (traditionally a highly anticipated and celebrated occasion among family).

I stared at my name and the church letterhead on the envelope. All eyes on me, I took a deep breath and opened the letter. I tried not to be dramatic as I read aloud, but I pronounced each word with deliberation—my hand covering the lines below. "Dear Elder Cook: You are hereby called to serve as a missionary of The Church of Jesus Christ of Latter-day Saints. You are assigned to labor in the Germany Leipzig Mission . . ." I was confounded—my silent pause seemed like an eternity. I just stared at the word *Leipzig*—it eerily seduced me from the page. I felt stunned—my surroundings became dim and muffled as I continued to read aloud, ". . . You will prepare to preach the gospel in the German language . . ." This enlivened my cognizance and I began to smirk. "What are ya gonna do?" they both asked in unison. I chuckled in disbelief, "I'm gonna go!" I was ecstatic—my brainchild had come into fruition and I felt pretty clever!

I was more infatuated than in love with Ed—I knew this because I wasn't willing to stay for him. He cried, begging me not to go, but I'm glad I was resolute enough to follow through. He was just coming out himself—and coming out like a storm. A super sexy, older, buff, steel mill worker, the cliché tall, dark, and handsome, he was a heartthrob. What made him so irresistible was his genteel nature; he, like myself, was a people-pleaser. I was taken aback while talking with mutual friends as we discovered that he was dating us simultaneously. Ironically, it was easy not to judge him. I understood somehow. Did I subconsciously sense that fidelity would not be my forté, either?

I was determined to get my free ride to Germany and then abandon it all to forge a new life as an expatriate. When the time approached, I got scared, so I called it off. As summer approached its end, I needed to decide whether to continue college or proceed with my mission. Staying in Idaho had run its course, and Germany's appeal enticed me unrelentingly. Germany represented the possibility of an exit and my escape into a new life. It beckoned me, and I was finally hopeful again!

WEST HOLLYWOOD

Two weeks before entering the Missionary Training Center, I went on a trip with Josh to West Hollywood. I had heard it was a gay mecca, and I wanted to fill up my reservoir before a long drought. We met up with another acquaintance from Idaho who turned out to be a sketchy influence, serving some warped agenda to pimp me out as a boy-toy. He tried to convince me of all the alluring grandeur and lifestyle of another nineteen-year-old who was allegedly employed already: the money, the clothes, the cars, the parties, the glitterati, and . . . and . . . and . . . For whatever reason, this guy did not want me going on my mission and did his best to persuade me otherwise. Something felt off about this guy—he barely knew me, yet seemed invested somehow in deterring me from my mission. We didn't have much conversation, but I sensed his own struggle—in his thirties, living off a "sugar daddy" and trying to make a name for himself as an extra (background actor). I was tempted and impressionable, but I questioned myself about the future and what would happen as I aged and got replaced. Thank God that I wasn't so naïve as to believe that being a "boy" would be my golden ticket. As I listened about the other boy lavishly squandering his money, I thought about his lack of savings, future job prospects, work experience, and education. I also wondered about his self-fulfillment and sense of personal pride. The only things attractive to me about his situation were the money and its opportunities, but that wasn't enough to cajole my own Faustian deal. I reconfirmed my resolve to continue with plan A.

Meanwhile, this acquaintance from Idaho had convinced me to go to a party, to which Josh was opposed. Josh always had my best interests at heart because he was a true friend, despite my immaturity and lack of respect. He trusted this guy and me to return home together. I was only nineteen, and they were in their thirties. I ended up going to that party and sleeping over with an actor. I don't remember the sex much, nor his status; I wouldn't have known, anyway, because I've never really followed pop culture or celebrities. I do remember, however, that he was gorgeous, his place was gorgeous, and, even if just for one night, he wanted *me*. I was nervous about not going home to where Josh and I were staying. I wasn't concerned for my own safety and well-being (though I should have been); rather, I knew that I had caused Josh to worry, and that was a shitty thing to do. I found my way back and arrived to a note reading that Josh had already left, driving back to Idaho. I felt like such a dick, but my fragile, just-inflated ego made it difficult for me to be humble enough for remorse. My erroneous behavior and disregard for Josh was embarrassing. Luckily for me, Josh returned to pick me up after he had already driven to Bakersfield, CA. Awkward silence accompanied us until after Vegas, when we finally spoke to each other. It killed me to sit in the discomfort of knowing I had disrespected and hurt Josh,—the only chance I had to salvage our friendship was to eat crow. "Josh . . . thank you for coming back . . . I'm sorry." I could barely muster with my head down. "How could you, knowing how I felt and worried about you?!" I had never seen Josh so upset. I felt like jumping out of the car, and secretly wished I was on a bus. I felt like shit for what I did, and it sucks to marinate in the aftermath of hurting someone's feelings. I was totally at his mercy. "Josh, please forgive me—I have no valid excuse." There was nothing more I could say to make it better. We cried.

I realized what a blessing it was to have good people in my life who really had my back. I've made amends with many friends throughout the years, but I still remember how bad it felt to treat them with disrespect and indecency. They've been generously kind and loving and deserved a much better friend than I was. Even though I didn't have the confidence to back it up, it was all about me—so selfish, so needy. I must have been such a drain . . . so self-absorbed. I can't even imagine which qualities kept good people in my life, with little return on their investment. My embarrassment serves as a reminder of unacceptable behavior as a decent person.

MISSIONARY
TRAINING CENTER

T ransitioning from the sinful pleasures of West Hollywood into the sterile and stark environment of the MTC was a jolt. I tried not to panic, but by then, I had basically pink-slipped myself into two months of daily projected rhetoric and supervised brainwashing. Everything was entirely regimented. A constant companion (another missionary in training) was mandatory 24/7, with no alone time except for in the bathroom. I'd wait to shower at night, right before curfew, because there were no private showers, just shower trees. Of course, I was still too shy and body conscious to shower with the others, but I also couldn't break my cover, and I knew that I'd eventually get caught staring in group showers. Besides, being the last person in the showers enabled me to sneak in a quick hand job.

I had to keep reminding myself of my goal, and knew I had to do whatever it took. It was the gateway to the liberty I envisioned for my life in Germany. I hid my secrets well. I was nineteen years old but wondered what it would be like to publicly date, to be nurtured in that arena by my family, friends, and community, and to mature into intimacy, instead of being suspect—shamed and judged by society at large (especially the Mormon faith). Was I to be driven into sneaky behavior as my only option for like-minded connections? What a vicious, self-perpetuating cycle!

As my anticipated departure approached, I progressively felt more revived, my exhilaration mitigating the rigid monotony of the MTC. Rumor had it that they needed to send a German-speaking missionary earlier than scheduled. I was pretty sure that it was going to be another Sister missionary who, contrary to my own falsified curriculum vitae, really did speak fluent German, and who had really lived in Germany. (Missionaries are given titles, followed by their last names; males are referred to as Elders, whereas female counterparts are called Sisters. For example, my name bar read "Elder Cook," as opposed to "Sister Cook.") While I was in class one day, I got summoned out over the intercom. Could it be that I was leaving early instead of her? I tried to contain my inner jubilation as my fellow missionaries in training gave me congratulatory looks. This had to be it! I was über-ready to go, counting down the days to help keep my sanity, knowing that I'd eventually exit that religious automaton factory. Had it not been for the intense rate of German instruction, I might have bailed of my own accord (gotten kicked out). I sat down in an office, and one of the church authorities uneasily informed me that they received a call from my church leader back home. Apparently, an entrusted ex-friend felt it her obligation to voice her concern against me. We had lost contact (by my design, as she had become needier than I could handle), and it felt conniving to me, given the fact that she wasn't privy to my life anymore. She must have seen the newspaper announcement about my mission. (It's common in Mormon communities to publish or celebrate departing and returning missionaries in local newspapers.) She betrayed things that I had told only to her in confidence back in high school. My disappointment in people increased, and this sting left a deep scar in my psyche.

The stakes were too high, and I had to deliver, so I profusely denied her accusations and invented a story about being sexually abused by adult men. Omitting my complicity in the matter, I lied. You can't abuse the willing, can you? I dredged up the tears and transformed my character into a victim. I had to convince him. Afterward, I was evaluated by a psychoanalyst—the gig was up. I had to answer a series of questions, take a personality test, and interpret pictures—along with recounting the impromptu victim story with emotional impact.

It was my ultimate audition—a feat that dumbfounded me . . . I was cleared to stay! Despite my ignoble deed, I was flush with confidence and was now emboldened for future duplicitous behavior.

MISSION ACCOMPLISHED

Had it not been for a few genuinely loving individuals, I would've bailed out of my mission (as planned) after getting settled in Germany. However, my mission president, his wife, and my training companion loved me despite my reluctance to adapt to missionary rules—especially time-management and leaving behind all other personal affairs. I did a lot out of love for them (like what I was supposed to be doing as a missionary) instead of dropping the ball altogether. My trainer was adorable, especially his soul. I wanted to rebel, but I didn't want to put him through the grief. We developed a bond and a brotherly love that totally disarmed me and derailed my plan. He was the consummate missionary and friend, full of love and service. When we were assigned new companions, I was devastated. My heart was broken, and I knew I couldn't comply with another like I did with him. I was integrating into the mission so much by this point that deserting posed a challenge to my emotional connections. Other missionaries who knew of my next companion eased my apprehension. Luckily, he was laid-back like they had said. I don't know if I talked him into letting me do my own thing (breaking mission rules, such as being alone) or if he just didn't care. In our new town, the church youth group was large, and we got along great. They even threw me a big birthday party with games, presents, and all. I couldn't remember the last time I was celebrated like that. I was quite in awe. Their inclusion of me kept me grounded, delaying my running away from the regimented system I'd blindly followed for so long. During one of my solo runs (a major no-no to venture alone), I encountered a man in the nearby woods watching me and masturbating. Of course I was intrigued, out of disbelief of what he was doing and also out of curiosity. We lived in a room on the top floor of a church member's home. Not long after engaging the interest of the man in the woods, he knocked on the door downstairs. I panicked and immediately sent him away. I was now paranoid and couldn't trust that he wouldn't come back. He definitely would blow my cover, so I called my mission president to report (without self-implication) that I was being stalked. I was transferred to another town shortly thereafter.

Beware of what you wish for—my next companion was an overt homophobe. We both knew about each other, as I found out that I was the talk of the mission. I wasn't shy about my "gay friendliness," and he was vocal about his disdain toward me. I overheard him complain to the mission president, asking what he had done wrong to deserve this. He was a numbers guy—consumed only by the statistics of the work, and not the meaning itself. If an investigator (a potential convert) showed no interest or progress toward baptism, he would drop him or her without hesitation. I knew what it felt like to be dropped. I wouldn't let him bully me into not visiting "eternal investigators" (those not committing to progress toward baptism). I also refused to preach anything in which I didn't myself believe. I remember proselytizing at a refugee asylum complex, and while visiting with one man, it was my turn to "bear testimony." I proclaimed a belief in something that wasn't my truth, "I know that Joseph Smith was a prophet, and that the *Book of Mormon* is true . . ." The hypocrisy felt like instant self-condemnation. I delivered conviction, but internally, I felt sick because I lied through my teeth—it was rehearsed. I had heard it all my life and it was easy to regurgitate the rhetoric.

My false preaching was poignant regret. I vowed to myself then and there never to preach anything with which I disagreed, so I pretty much befriended our contacts and left any preaching and/ or testimony bearing to my companions. This companion and I tolerated each other because we had to, but it was a long, forced two months together. We both were more than ready and happy when transfers came (transfers are when the mission reshuffles companions and places within the mission).

I prodded to get to know the people because I sought authentic connection. Paradoxically, by selfishly indulging in the lives of others, I lost myself in service to them. I didn't feel deceptive, like I was baiting them, because I sincerely wanted to know their stories, to get to the heart of our shared humanity. I didn't want to feel like a Charlatan, so I had faith that I could only bring out the best in myself and others by having no agenda. My personal mission was to connect and feel, to develop love and forget myself.

I was thrilled to be paired up with my last companion, especially because we had cheered and competed together at Nationals '98. He was an Adonis, and I had to divert my lust because we worked well together and I didn't want to muddy the waters. He became fodder for fantasies as I masturbated—also a major no-no—in the shower, the only way I could get away with it.

It seems like when life wants to teach a lesson, it's gentle at first and then crescendos with each avoidance. I was bombarded by messages about integrity and the freedom and happiness it enables. One particular Sunday at church, every message hit home and felt personally aimed at me. I was overcome with emotion by an overwhelming source of love—my personal affirmation that I was okay—that I was meant to be myself! After church, I locked myself in our bathroom, stared at my reflection in the mirror and cried. I was tired of keeping up my web of compounding lies for survival, tired of managing my secrets . . . it was wreaking havoc on my psyche. I realized that I couldn't personally grow anymore until I came clean with my own conscience. Knowing that being gay wasn't an issue with God set me free to discover my true potential as a compassionate soul intertwined with the universe as a whole. I was ready to be courageous. I called my mission president and confessed my deceit. He asked to meet with me right away. I told my companion that I'd probably be leaving soon but that I wanted him to know how much he meant to me, being my friend. He hugged me and told me he was proud of me "manning up," knowing that the immediate road ahead would be treacherous. We hugged and cried.

I faced immense ridicule, judgment, and disappointment, but for the first time in my life, I was proud, courageous, and redeemed from my own trappings. I knew that I was good with God, and nothing else mattered! This liberation carried me through the challenges ahead. The plane ride home was peaceful. I kept staring out the window—proud of myself, yet humbled by my surrender. I was the last one off the plane, and as I walked down the jet bridge, I got excited for a joyful reunion with my parents at the gate (1999). I lit up when I saw them, but the emotional grief on their faces made me feel like I brutally bludgeoned their hopes. They were so distraught. I wanted desperately to have them happily welcome me home with anticipation, but the disappointment that I felt from my family in general was palpable. I was on my own. My mission president wanted me to stay in Germany, but the powers that be in Salt Lake City demanded my immediate return. The night of my arrival back home, I was stripped of my "powers and privileges" as a missionary and greeted with a formal letter "inviting" me to attend my own church court trial to be held five days later. I had prepared for this event years in advance. It haunted me, but now I was ready. I practically welcomed it.

MORMON NO MORE

I don't believe in excommunication, but I knew that I needed a clean break to avoid being harassed by the Mormon church in the future. It was intimidating walking into that room of fifteen church leaders and authorities. I was guilty until proven innocent. The inquisition was brutal, and the scrutinizing interrogation was hyper-intrusive and relentless. These strangers among acquaintances were privy to my most personal and vulnerable history. I wondered if some of them (all men) actually got off on hearing all my lurid, detailed sexual escapades? My privacy was violated as my soul was stripped and exposed. The sanctimonious stake president had threatened me before I went on my mission not to come home early and disgrace him. (A stake is a group of several smaller congregations called wards, which are presided over by individual bishops.) He did not want his image tarnished. Ultimately, he had the final say, and I had a feeling that he was out for revenge, disguised as "revelation from God." This self-righteous human on a power trip would judge me and deliver my comeuppance. Regardless of the outcome, I was at peace, and I felt powerful. The men adjourned for forty-five minutes to deliberate my verdict. I sat alone in silence and surrender as I waited for my fate, which would change the course of my life and affect my family. (Eternal families in the hereafter are contingent on worthy church membership). I was excommunicated, in the name of God.

I was granted permission to quote my former home-ward bishop, who witnessed my excommunication process. I've had loving conversations with him and his wife, and their friendship, especially when they had no obligation and it would have been easier not to be my friends, still means so much to me. He was the only loving person who boldly took a stand against the injustice, who didn't judge my actions, but knew my heart. The cards were already stacked against me as a gay Mormon, so I learned the rules and played the cards that I was dealt the best way I knew how, given my circumstances. It was a zero-sum game: I could either stay true to myself and lose everything else (family, friends, community, social structure, school, etc.), or win at their game and lose myself. I don't beat myself up over surviving and coping by any means necessary; rather, I thank my resourcefulness in taking care of myself. The system failed me. The following confirmed my experience:

> I thought they would be loving and forgiving once they heard from you, but, instead, they could only think of punishment. When given an opportunity to speak on your behalf, I tried to defend you and indicated what a wonderful young man you were, but it appeared that no one was interested in any of my comments. When a vote was taken to sustain President [name undisclosed]'s decision to excommunicate you from the church, I was the only person to vote against his proposal. Everyone else voted to sustain his decision. President [name undisclosed] indicated that he would proceed without my support. A church court is supposed to be a court of love, not of punishment. I felt that the decision was wrong then and I continue to believe that the stake president rushed to judgment and made a terrible mistake.—T.L.

This solidified my resolve to take my spirituality into my own hands. Having no more middlemen was liberating but scary. I had to take full responsibility and accountability for what I believed in or didn't—no more blaming, no more playing the victim, no more following or subjecting myself to brainwashing. Blind faith in my defunct belief system had not served me well. The tragic flaw of believing in a religious institution that didn't believe in me stunted my spirituality. Sadly, I also let my personal development become arrested. I felt duped. My family was devastated by my religious shunning, especially my parents. I was crushed. No one commended my courage. I felt abandoned, dealing with the unknown ahead of me all alone. I was in uncharted territory. Excommunication was so taboo in Mormonism that even as prepared as I was, I felt lost. Without direction, identity, or support, I was afraid and lonely.

I only wanted someone to hug me, to tell me that it would be okay, that I'd be okay, and to acknowledge what it took to face the fire! I just wanted to be loved, just because, as I was, and not for whom I was expected to be. I had to fight my relentless self-critic from the rhetorical belief that I was "less than," not good, not enough. How was I supposed to love God—or even my fellow man—if I wasn't allowed my own self-acceptance, -worth, and -love? I was reticent about the hypocrisy. I had trusted them. I had trusted my family's belief system. I was failed. All my fears, hopes, and feelings of desperation I had to cope with on my own. My anxiety manifested itself in many forms of compulsion and obsession, including visible signs on my body. Self-destructively, I yearned to feel better and escape my mental torment by any means, no matter what. My quest to ameliorate my lack perpetuated my deficit. The temporary, empty remedies of sex, alcohol, and codependency left me feeling worse.

What if I had had the support I needed when I needed it most?!

PERFECT MORMON

L et me pretend like everything's perfect, because that's the way it should be, right? If it's not, then it must be my fault— unwilling to be humble and give up my personal power to the controlling, dogmatic dictates. How dare they claim my dignity and make me dependent, codependent, and cowardly! I remember an innocent Billy Ray, who was beaten down and broken into an insecure and lost soul. Was I going to hell? Hadn't I already experienced a version of it?!

I regret that I gave my power away to others and let them rule my life. I was such a passive people-pleaser, but I had to learn the hard way to say no—no to surrendering to their control, no to acquiescing to condescension and inferiority, no to following blindly, no to invalidating myself. They had owned me.

Why? For my 10 percent tithing?! It didn't feel right—giving them money before, when I could help my sister instead, so that's what I did. At the end of each year, the Mormon church has a series of scheduled one-on-one interviews called Tithing Settlement. It's kind of like their final roundup to coerce full payment of any oversights, usually accompanied with propaganda reinforcing compliance. During mine one year as a young teenager, long before I was on their radar, the bishop inquired about why I wasn't tithing, to which I responded that I was indeed. He invalidated my contributions to my sister, claiming that "the church" knew best how to help her. Even after my excommunication, they tried to coerce my tithing—with precondition that it not be received from me directly but by proxy through a "worthy member," such as my mom. Imagine the gall!

All of the lies and condemnation about homosexuality stunted my development into the intelligent, self-confident, independent freethinker I was destined to become. God, how irresponsibly gullible I was, my trust and self-esteem exploited—the damage! I don't know how, but I at least kept my spark, my lust for life. Are they even aware of the degradation caused by labeling people as sinners, as not good enough? My questioning was discouraged when I didn't accept "their" answers. According to them, naturally, the truth would've been revealed to me had I not hardened my heart and challenged authority—heaven forbid! I'd cry myself to sleep, depressed and hating myself. I entertained the simplicity of committing suicide, but my belief in a hell worse than the one I'd already been assigned deterred me. No hope. No happiness. No peace. How sad! What a ruthless institution, getting people to succumb to the dogma, brainwashing from the get-go. I wish that I hadn't been pigeonholed into that belief system.

I wanted to be safe by avoiding risks, but moreover, I didn't want to live a blasé, mediocre life. I didn't want my life to be a buzzkill. I have an inherent optimism, too precious to compromise for any moral checklists. Their scrutinizing, judgmental standards are no longer mine. No more conformity. To hell with perfection, that impossible ideal that robbed my peace and sanity for so much of my life! My contentment is a byproduct of accepting my humanity, along with all its imperfections. My faith in divine grace edifies me.

I'm grateful for my release from the Mormon institution, and I celebrate my liberation. It was the green light for me to discover myself, to start living my own life, and to eventually invest in my spirituality. I know that everything coalesced into becoming who

I am today. I own it proudly. As reluctant as I was to feel through the pain, cultivating a joyful life is invaluable.

Thank you, Martha Beck, for your powerful memoir, *Leaving the Saints: How I Lost the Mormons and Found My Faith.*

PETER

I was supposed to meet a friend at the Memphis Pyramid Arena for a multilevel-marketing business convention, but I wasn't able to find her, and I had no cell phone. I walked to the police station to use their phone to search for nearby motel or hostel vacancy, but none had any. I was stranded, so I hailed a cab to the nearest gay bar, figuring that that would be my best bet for finding help. I waited, sitting atop the sidewalk wall. I soon found out it was a leather bar, so I really stuck out—dapper in slacks, a white shirt, and a tie. They probably thought I was some high-end rent-boy. I didn't feel comfortable addressing the men leaving—except for one man about to cross the street. I didn't really have a good reason why I was drawn to him in particular, other than my intuition, but I sensed the urge to speak with him. I chickened out, though, and was disappointed in myself for missing my opportunity. I watched him get into his car and pull out onto the road from the parking lot. He stopped, made a U-turn and pulled up to me with the passenger window down. He asked if I was okay, and I said that I needed help. I only had a hundred dollars on me with no credit card and nowhere to stay. He offered to let me stay at his place, and I got into his car feeling relieved and safe.

As we lay in bed, he listened to my whining and bitterness about my negative Mormon experiences and familial difficulties. He sympathized and comforted me. I let him fuck me, thinking that it was the least I could do to repay his kindness. I would give it up (my body) out of gratitude and as the only thing I thought that I had to offer in exchange for attention and validation from men. I felt empty.

I remember the mockingbird outside his place. I was amazed at how it mimicked Peter's whistle—just like I mimicked expectations that others had of me. Whenever my family mentioned my strong testimony of Mormonism, in essence, they complimented my then ability to execute that role. I was far removed on the inside from what I convinced others to believe on the outside. The more I wanted to hide, the more I overcompensated.

Back home, I received an inscribed book in the mail from Peter, *The Language of Letting Go* by Melody Beattie—it would become my new *Book of Mormon*.

AACHEN

I missed Germany and didn't want to be back in Idaho. I felt condemned and ostracized. So I applied online to become an au pair. The process was much faster than I expected, and I returned to Germany within months. The parents knew I was gay, and my mission president gave them high praise and recommendation of me when they contacted him for my reference. I was excited to return, this time as a civilian. I was nervous, but my parents seemed proud of my new endeavor.

The mother and her two sons picked me up in Brussels, and the hour drive to Aachen was a little uncomfortable as we tried to get to know each other. The family was über-wealthy—the father owning major flea markets, and the mother a renowned urologist. They had transformed a former castle into their family home. It was gargantuan, with my room directly below the tower. After I got settled in, the mother took me on a walk around the grounds near the forest, explaining my duties and her expectations of me. She asked if I'd be willing to exchange some of my time off for a little extra money. I trusted that my compensation would be equitable.

I didn't realize it at the time, but I was denying my pain from being exiled, excommunicated from my foundation. My public identity had been revoked, and I was vulnerable, impressionable, and willing to do anything in order to be accepted. I was not only the nanny, but also the housekeeper, chauffeur, and groundskeeper.

I was back to square one, having traded religious servitude for domestic servility. I allowed myself to be exploited. I didn't know any better until I met Nate and Jared. I heard that there was a gay couple who owned a coffee shop/delicatessen nearby, so of course I had to check it out, hoping to meet them. I first met Nate, who invited me to their home for dinner. We all hit it off splendidly, and I ended up spending my one-day weekends with them. They gradually learned of my situation as I revealed my troubles and frustration. They became concerned and furious, so they started teaching me how to stand up for myself.

I formulated a work plan—reducing my weekly work load from sixty to forty-five hours—still giving them the upper hand, as our original contract stated only thirty-five hours. My extra twenty-five hours only profited me fifty German marks. For a long time, when I thought about how exploitive that was, I resented them—and myself for letting them take advantage of me. I presented my plan, but to no avail. They said it would require them to hire another employee, which they refused to do.

At that point, I was contemplating moving in with Nate and Jared into the top floor apartment of their four-story home. Shortly after my attempt to ameliorate my work situation, I was riding with the mother to pick up one of the boys from an activity, and in the car, he asked if he could visit me on weekends if I moved out. I answered that he'd have to ask his parents, but that I'd be happy for him to visit. When we arrived back at the house, after he had gone upstairs, she closed the doors behind him. "When you leave here, I don't want you contacting the kids." she said callously. "What the . . . ?!" I wondered stupefied. Her remarks shattered my fragile, hollow shell of a self because I was so dependent on her acceptance and approval. I let her define me and determine my self-worth. "You'll never be independent, because you can't accomplish anything on your own." she beat me down even more. Any puny spark of confidence that I had developed was extinguished—believing that I didn't have what it took to be successful in life.

I had developed a special bond with the kids, especially the two boys, ages nine and twelve. I was more like a fun big brother than a disciplinarian. I guess that stemmed from my own upbringing, being the baby of six. My parents weren't too strict with me, but then again, I didn't give them reason to be (of which they knew). I spent a lot of time with the boys and loved them like my own nephews. The way they looked up to me meant the world. I was jealous of the parents getting all the credit, but how could I blame the kids for wanting love, affection and attention from their parents (other than for show at grandiose parties)? Was it all just obliged showcase pretense? The affectation was repulsive.

Before I emotionally broke down, I asked for the rest of the day off, internally gutted and knowing that I was useless at that point. I was desperate, so I clung to her only reassuring, final words that I was the best nanny for the boys. She finally acknowledged my beneficial influence and admitted her satisfaction with its positive impact on their behavior. I went into a storage room out back, shut the door and slid to the floor, bawling uncontrollably. I didn't know what to do. After I mustered some composure, I called a friend back home and then my parents. They verbalized their love and support and their belief in me. Their encouragement was my hope. I felt at rock bottom, but didn't want to go back home to Idaho, and I knew I couldn't stay in that house—nor did I want to. Although I was still employed with room and board, I couldn't allow myself to be victimized anymore.

I had the epiphany that the choice was mine: either to believe the mother and let my life spiral into self-destruction, or to prove her wrong, for my own sake. Eventually, I was able to forgive her when I realized how much of a catalyst she was in making me take the risk to believe in myself and what a gift that was for my future. I believe that the universe had bigger plans for me than to allow my complacency in another system of conformity. As scary as it seems, the courage it takes to believe in yourself not only liberates you, but also empowers your best life. I could have easily let myself self-destruct as a victim, but I chose to find out my true mettle— to reclaim the power that I had surrendered to those who had usurped control over me. Even though I felt alone with no sense of self or belonging, I started packing. I wrote individual farewell letters, left them on the kitchen counter, and took pictures of the kids sleeping. I moved out during the night.

Nate and Jared were the fulcrum I needed to develop my self-confidence beyond just surviving tumultuous events, and were monumental for my personal growth and development. They helped me filter my brainwashed psyche and taught me how to start enjoying life. I had to learn self-respect by unlearning self-sabotaging beliefs. For the first time in my life, I was celebrating my sexuality—starting to enjoy sex for what it is without the self-torture of internalized guilt and shame. They wine-and-dined me, traveled with me, and showed me a new way of living free of judgment and pressure. I finally felt free to let loose and have fun, and have fun I did.

I sought out the adult bookstore, having habituated myself to such locales back in Idaho and Utah. The bookstores offered opportune access to like-minded people and the potential for sex. Still being controlled by the grip of ingrained guilt and shame stemming from puritanical religion and reinforced by American taboos, I was hesitant to enter, but my curiosity and hormones took over. I might have seemed like I knew what I was doing, but my nerves were screaming inside! I was the proverbial kid in a candy store, but this time I wasn't in Idaho anymore! The porn shelves led to the video cabin halls—dark and full of roaming men groping themselves, eye-fucking me. I'm pretty sure they honed in on my vulnerability, so I entered the porn theater as a temporary escape and an opportunity to arrange my thoughts for my next move.

My faux confidence could only mask so much, so I found the nearest exit. A man sitting in his car stared at me, and feeling familiar with car cruising, I felt less tense than I was inside the building. He motioned for me to approach and to get in. I asked where he was from, detecting a non-German accent. He said, "Yugoslavia," and I concluded he didn't want to give specifics, as Yugoslavia didn't exist anymore. He asked if I wanted to fuck him. I don't remember him being ugly, but even if he was, I probably would have said yes anyway. I wanted exotic experiences and felt ugly inside, so the situation didn't call any self-respect into question. We drove to a secluded, run-down, and vacant industrial lot. I thought to myself, "I could be raped, killed, or both, and no one would find me, nor be able to identify me." Still maintaining my naïve trust in strangers, I put the thought out of my head. He was snorting some white powder and asked if I wanted any, but I declined. I figured it was expensive when I accidentally brushed some onto the floor and he started freaking out. Sensing my cluelessness, he calmed down after sniffing something out of a bottle to "relax" him. He used spit to lube his ass, then sat on my dick, sliding up and down, facing forward as he squatted over me as I sat in the front passenger seat. While he rode my dick, snorting and sniffing, his cell phone rang. As he answered, I thought, "Is this really happening?" From his end of the conversation, I gathered that it was his wife, upset about him being late and asking where he was and when he'd be home. He also spoke with his young daughter. I started to feel uglier inside, especially after he defecated on the ground outside the door. I was disgusted—with myself, with my participation, with all aspects of that scenario. My own culpability warranted no judgment from myself toward him.

Being demonized as a gay sinner warped my emotional maturity, and I had no paradigm of a healthy gay life. Years of self-deprecating beliefs take their toll and stifle hopeful, enlightened, and empowered living. Any sense of sexual expression was shamed—a recipe for sordid encounters. I wanted sex. What twenty-one-year-old male doesn't?! Sadly, I didn't know how to get it without compromising who I was. I hitchhiked one night, hoping for more than just a ride. A man picked me up and took me to his apartment. Again, not taking into account the risk, I was proactively complicit. His apartment was dirty with clutter, some piled or scattered, furniture in disarray. His mattress was on the floor. I was more leery about the cleanliness of his mangled sheets than I was about my physical safety. As we fucked like wild animals, I smirked with pleasure: the way it felt, our reflections in the mirrors—like watching ourselves star in our own live porn, the sound of sweaty bodies slapping against each other. Mostly, I reveled in the defiance of my religious upbringing that had made me feel "less than." The fact that I was a former missionary now enjoying the ecstatic charge of raw, carnal hedonism intensified the sweet savor of that forbidden fruit. I wanted all my self-righteous church leaders to witness this deliberate "Fuck you!"

Salacious sex in foreign languages with foreigners abroad was an item on my list that I checked off with proud satisfaction. Now that I was more confident in my sexuality as far as sex itself was concerned, the opportunities almost consumed me. The lustful allure of it all beckoned me, and I wanted to be defiled. Unbridled pleasures and debauchery seemed inconsequential and my craving insatiable as I glorified my assimilation. I felt deprived—some would say depraved, but I had no shame. The pendulum was swinging from self-effacement to self-absorption. Sure it was fun, but truth be told, what it all boiled down to was buried pain and unhealed wounds.

Not long after moving into the upstairs apartment, I moved down into the main house with Nate and Jared, sharing their bed. We developed into a threesome relationship, and to our pleasant surprise, our dynamics worked swimmingly, despite minor miscommunication due to language barriers. No English was spoken, and Jared only spoke French, so I spoke German with Nate and became emotionally attached to him. Wanting to stay in Germany, I was hired to paint apartments and wash dishes in their bakery during the day and completed German night courses to earn my official German certificate.

I had applied to and been accepted by the University of Cologne to study Romance languages. Unfortunately, my self-confidence wasn't yet strong enough to fully expatriate at the age of twenty-one. Also, Nate and Jared were more invested in me than I wanted to reciprocate. I was still a people-pleaser and too cowardly to communicate that I didn't want our threesome to continue long-term, so I used my ticket home at the end of the year as my plausible exit.

Germany had enriched my life and taught me to appreciate the importance of meaningful connections, the fun of socializing, and the peace of relaxing—but most importantly, I started to believe in myself and develop self-confidence. I treasure the gifts of my coming-of-age experience. I couldn't absorb enough. I miss those special dinners with our group of friends lasting into the wee hours of morning as we enjoyed each other's company, conversation, food, and drink. I have fond memories of glorious afternoons spent strolling different locations, basking in the sun, taking in the splendid scenic beauty of both land- and cityscape, and interacting with the locals in their own tongue. I was creating a new identity, and it thrilled me that German was the language of my personal renaissance. Gratitude brought me to tears.

PARTY-AND-PLAY

T he sadness of saying good-bye to Germany and what it
represented to me was affronted by the culture shock of
being back in America. The juxtaposition depressed me.
Luckily, Memphis and New Orleans offered to add continued
novel experiences to my repertoire, but May was approaching, and
I didn't want to bear the heat and humidity of the summer months
in the south. I used the example of other dancers getting involved
with drugs, porn, or prostitution as my excuses to leave Bourbon
Street. In retrospect, though, I left because I had developed a
positive enough body image to not want to be objectified for money
anymore. Plus, I needed another challenge—another geographical
cure. Too bad I didn't yet understand that my penchant for
wanderlust was doubling as a coping mechanism. Although it
satisfied my appetite for novelty, it was only a temporary placebo
for my unhealed soul. Geographical cures, like sexual quick
fixes, neither cured nor fixed what I was trying to run from or
anesthetize: myself. So I had the brilliant idea to go back to school
in Idaho for the advantage of in-state tuition.

I should've known better. It didn't take long before I was
spinning my wheels again. I wanted something more. Like in
George Michael's *Flawless*, I wanted to "go to the city"—any city
that would offer me more than minimum wage, with possibilities
of dreaming bigger for myself. I was tired of living a blasé life of
obscurity in Idaho. By chance, I was invited by a friend, Spencer,

to see Cirque du Soleil's *Mystère* in Vegas with him. I was in total awe at the grace and movement of the human body exhibited throughout the show. I daydreamed of how amazing it would be to be a performing artist. After the show, we were invited to a private dinner reception. During conversation, Spencer received a phone call from his friend in Vegas, asking if he knew of someone to be a replacement dancer for *The Folies Bergère* show. Knowing that I could tumble, he suggested me, and we left immediately to go to their stage to audition. Luckily, I had my running shoes and a pair of shorts in the car.

I impressed them with my round-off back-hand-spring full-twist. I nailed it! However, my dancing skills weren't as fluid. I felt clumsy, struggling through an impromptu routine that they tried to teach me right after my tumbling pass. I saw the dismay on their faces, and I knew that they were torn. They wanted my tumbling but needed my dancing. They hesitantly said yes, and I got a chunk of hair cut off of my head the next day for drug testing. I was elated—I was really going to be a Vegas performer! I couldn't stop imagining the fun, the money, and the exposure. I gave two weeks' notice at both my jobs. I was on my way to bigger and better.

A representative from the show called me, informing me that their original dancer resigned his contract. I was in shock. What was I going to do?! I had no jobs to go back to, and my ego was too bruised to admit my folly in rushing into something so fickle as the entertainment industry. I couldn't go back to Idaho, but I didn't know how to stay in Vegas.

Humiliated, I asked Josh in Salt Lake if I could stay with him until I got back on my feet. Fortunately, I found temp work right away and eventually a nice, well-paying job at the exclusive Alta Club, which enabled me to continue school in Utah.

However, I still had hopes of being part of that wild, alluring world I had glimpsed in Vegas. Meanwhile, Spencer had moved from Idaho back to Vegas (where he's from), so I drove down to visit him. He was living with a friend who had his own Vegas show and seemed well connected. The three of us went to see *Chippendale's*. Not only was it eye candy galore, but I also knew that I could dance like them. It reminded me of a mix between cheer dance and strip dance. I wanted to be one of them! Spencer's friend said that he could get me an audition, and the exhilaration came back—I thought I had another chance. After the show, I was invited into the friend's room. He wanted to "party-and-play" with me (do drugs and have sex). The forty-five-year age difference wasn't an issue, but he looked so abnormally haggard with mileage. I'm usually pretty generous when it comes to rating good looks, but I couldn't even go to a happy place in my mind in order to go through with it. He took my rejection in stride—or so I thought, until I never heard from him again. I had sent him a thank-you card and left messages thanking him for the show, but I was slow to realize the rude awakening of how some opportunities were had in Vegas: the implicit and proverbial casting couch. I identified again with George Michael's *Flawless*—I was "more than just some fucked-up piece of ass!"

I started frequenting Vegas on weekends to visit Spencer, and we would do crystal meth and fuck random guys all weekend. I trusted him. He was about twenty-five years my senior and was down-to-earth. Even though he had his own bragging rights, he was always humble about his looks and accomplishments as a model and actor. "Tina," as the drug is nicknamed, is horrendously dangerous and destructive, but I was naïve and felt invincible. With Tina, I had no need for sleep and no appetite, and I could have sex for days without losing any gusto. All my sexual hang-ups disappeared under its influence. However, not being able to cum was frustrating. The worst, though, was the inevitable crash afterward—terrible Tuesdays! Absolutely dreadful. Misery was the price I paid for quick fixes.

Still, it thrilled me to do naughty things—each was another "Fuck you!" to the conventions that had stifled me. Mormon oppression had left me marinating in residual bitterness, and I disdainfully regret not choosing to do better. I wouldn't be able to change or improve until I acknowledged the gift of the lesson and recognized my own culpability.

I'm extremely lucky and thank the universal powers that be that I escaped addiction to crystal methamphetamine. There are horror stories of lives ruined by it—people controlled and taken over by chemicals; their health, relationships, livelihoods, and credibility all destroyed; their possessions and, ultimately, their lives lost. Naïveté is no excuse anymore, and I try to live a good life as gratitude for not falling victim to the chemicals in which I dabbled.

ANDY

I used the gym as an escape from my insecurities and as a distraction from dealing with my issues. Endorphins became my drug of choice, and I craved the rush that I felt after every hit of running. During one of my runs, I noticed a tall, handsome silver fox pass by, and I thought to myself, *Out of my league.* He had a great smile, along with a toned, muscular body. After my run, I got a tingle inside when I saw him again in the locker room. My mind raced with lust. Instead of pursuing him, my intuition prompted me to just be. We had a pleasant introductory conversation. His name was Andy, and I felt that he was a good guy with substance. I desperately needed friends who cared about me without sexual agenda. Our friendship evolved naturally as we shared mutual trust and vulnerability. We had a common background regarding Mormon families, being gay and out of the faith, and failed attempts to reconcile the conflict.

I didn't express it to Andy, but I was emotionally falling in love with him. I didn't tell him because I knew that I'd be relocating soon to New York City for my new job as a JetBlue flight attendant. I also was scared to let go of the familiarity and comfort of the status quo.

Not only was Andy kind and sexy, but the sex was amazing as well. He eased me into trying things of my own volition and curiosity—things I didn't know if I'd even like. I vividly remember him walking into the room, the epitome of masculinity, his body hair patterned perfectly over his muscles and his gorgeous, thick, long cock against his low-hanging balls. I practically melted. Submission came easily as he tied my hands behind my back and fucked me as my face pushed into the pillow. He pulled out and his cum shot over my head, warmly splatting onto my back. My orgasm was intense! In the outdoor shower, the warm sun glistened off our wet, naked bodies. Although being pee shy, I was intrigued, so he persuaded me to piss on him as he knelt at my feet. Then, kneeling at his feet and looking up at his strapping, Tom-of-Finland body, I felt his piss hit my chest and trickle down into the crevices of my nether regions. Never say never.

DOWN-LOW

L iving in Salt Lake, I developed an unhealthy association with married men. The majority of my sexual exploration was with Mormon men—men who kept their activities secret from their wives and families, still going to church on Sundays and wearing their holy garments. For many of them, I was their first dalliance with another man. It flattered me, made me feel valued, good enough, sexy enough for a "straight" man to risk so much. We would spend most of our time together simply talking. I felt honored that they would confide in me and feel comfortable enough to do so. I respected that they were letting their guard down. I didn't take their trust in me lightly, and I prided myself on confidentiality. I've been the holder of many secrets, many never-before-disclosed confessions, and I consider that a huge compliment. I understand vulnerability.

Their body language emanated apprehension yet longing for male intimacy. They were enthralled with the attention I paid to every part of their bodies as I talked them through their fears and insecurities. In essence, I felt like a coach—or the instructor of Married Men on the Down-Low 101. I knew how vulnerable the experience could be and made sure we communicated beforehand—I never wanted them to do anything that they didn't want to do. Some of them got emotional, sharing forbidden intimacy but enslaved to fear. My initial rush of sexual excitement transformed into help mode. Questions about their mental and emotional states flooded my mind. I knew the disconnect far too well. I justified being "the other man" with the rationale that I was helping them somehow—to facilitate their own quick fixes in order to spice up their sex lives at home, to release their pent-up whatever so they could refocus on their commitments, to let them vent, etc. I remembered how important it was to me when others had listened to my confessions, frustrations, and tribulations and how cathartic it was to get things out of my head. I'd like to think that I was being altruistic with those married men, but I guess that we all helped each other fulfill unmet needs, sexually and emotionally. I'm grateful that my life course steered me away from such a similar trajectory of masked identity. I'm glad that I chose to create an authentic life how I wanted before rushing into those life-altering decisions, commitments, and responsibilities.

HEATH

Becoming a flight attendant and living in Manhattan was exhilarating! I had initiated correspondence with an older man online, as I was seeking a room/-mate in Manhattan. We decided to meet for dinner, and we clicked. His name was Heath, and he was an investment banker from London. Jovial banter and shared intellectual curiosity kept us both interested in developing a friendship. Having lived in Europe myself and being up-to-date on world current events, I was able to hold my own with ease, and I think that he was pleasantly surprised. At the end of our rendezvous, he offered me his place, rent-free, in exchange for only upkeep and utilities. It was a spacious, one-bedroom apartment with its own private courtyard. I was in shock. I knew that it was one of those seldom, serendipitous opportunities, so I gratefully accepted. If I was going to live in New York, why not do it right? He flew me out to London for a week of lavish living, accentuated with cocaine-laced parties and dancing.

Exploring on my own, I found myself in Saint Paul's Cathedral. I was living on a high of all the new and exciting changes in my life, but my familial and romantic relationships were in limbo. Sitting on a bench inside, I started to pray. Tears streamed down my face as I tacitly asked God to help me find peace in uncertainty. I felt viscerally relieved of anxiety and conflict. I had to live my life and let others love me or leave me.

I had two consecutive boyfriends, albeit briefly: the first a prominent businessman, the second a former Olympic speed-skater turned Olympic speed-skating coach. Appearances made it seem like I had it all put together, but luxurious living can't heal a broken soul. They both dumped me, and the rejection shattered my delicate, shallow self. I broke down bawling in front of the mirror, not liking how I felt inside, not liking my lack of character, not liking my dependence on external validation. I grabbed my cell phone, sunk to the floor against my bed, and wept while I scrolled through each contact, sobbing, "I don't need you! I don't need you!" It was painful, because even though the truth was that I didn't need them, the daunting work of learning to like my own company felt overwhelming. I went through with all of the deletions, knowing that I had to start needing myself more. Who was I? What was I worth?

Several months later, serendipity led me to meet Kirk, my love, life partner, and best friend. I fell in love with his kind soul, amplified by his sexy good looks. I had forgotten how to be myself, and with him, I was getting my glow back. In the interim, Heath had found his husband-to-be. I met him once, and since then, I lost all contact with them. His partner was the epitome of royal wealth, pomp, and arrogance—too refined in his own eyes to appreciate commoners' humanity. He was quite the dainty flower. Heath became negligent with the rent, and my attempts to contact him were all callously snubbed. My assumption is that his partner felt threatened by my friendship with Heath, who is thirty years my senior. I didn't stay at the apartment when Heath was in town, and we didn't have a sexual relationship. My conclusion is that he became an abject yes-man to his new husband. I lost a lot of respect for Heath. I thought that he was stronger than that, especially given his status in the professional world.

AUSTIN

I went out dancing with Kirk in Austin. Observing the crowd from a balcony above the dance floor, I imagined the coming out stories of the guys and gals below. I wondered what my story would have been like under different circumstances. Was it as hard for others as I felt it was for me? Were they as terrified and anxious as I was? Did they struggle with self-image, family, clergy, friends, or identity? Did they struggle at all? At least at that moment, as the music entranced us to move to the beat, life felt enchanted—I was having fun with Kirk, who loves me. I didn't have to vie for attention or worry about rejection. I was able to just be, and enjoy it. Younger and older alike, all were sexy. We all seemed to be having fun, exuding neither pretense nor attitude. I wasn't worried about body image or acceptance. I was lost in the euphoria of the music and dancing. I even approached one of the guys dancing on the stage (whose good looks normally would have intimidated me) to compliment his smile and sexiness. He thanked me and to my surprise said that it meant a lot to him because he considered the other guys on the stage sexier than him. More and more, I realize that the human experience is universal—that we're our own worst critics. We all seek inclusion and acceptance. Who *doesn't* like feeling sexy and wanted? I thrive on attention.

PALM SPRINGS

irk and I got together with two other couples for a friends' vacation in Palm Springs. Our time there coincided with Saint Patrick's Day weekend, so festivities were brewing. We went to the local gay bar for some drinks and fun. The music was invigorating, the men were beautiful, and the dancing transported me to a euphoric high. We made our way to the lounge bar, and our attention was captivated by the scantily clad, gorgeous dancers on their boxes, suggestively dancing and flirting, consenting to be touched for money. I had flashbacks to my dancing days in the Big Easy. I wondered about the internal dialogue they might have been having and whether it was like my own when I was in their boots at age twenty-two. It was interesting for me to observe, having now had the experience on both sides.

It's rare to find a dancer who actually dances and converses with their clientele as equals. I immediately noticed such a dancer and was intrigued to test my assumptions. As we conversed, I learned that we both were thirty years old and that he too was Mormon. However, unlike myself, he was married and still going through the temple (a select privilege reserved solely for the "worthy"). He loved the attention, but I was sorry he was going down that road—the same one that I had been destined to follow, that road of marriage as a closeted gay man, that road where so many don't dare to be themselves. What were *his* substitutes for love?

I was glad to see him really dancing like I had, having sincerely enjoyed the music whether I got tipped or not. Sincerity shines through and is highly attractive—plus confidence is super sexy! It bothered me, though, that he was deceiving himself, his wife, and his family. I saw in him what I disliked in myself back then. I wanted to test his devotion to the Mormon faith, so upon saying good-bye, I reached out my hand and gave him the "secret handshake," only revealed to those worthy elite who go through the temple. It's part of a choreographed ritual that grants you admission through the veil between the spirit world and heaven after death. He immediately jerked his hand away, being freaked out. Was it my place to merge his two identities? How could I judge him when I had gone through the same process? A double life is difficult to reconcile!

CHRIS

I was in Florida for a weekend and wanted to go to the beach, but it was raining and windy. I decided to go to the gay bathhouse to enjoy its amenities. Later, as the sun broke through the clouds, I took advantage of the calm by relaxing by the outdoor pool. Lying across from me was a stunningly sexy man with all the perfect features that one would expect of a model in magazines. His build wasn't bulky, but his muscles were well defined and toned. I thought for sure he would have the attitude to match, and I considered him untouchable—out of my league to even approach.

I don't remember how I struck up a conversation with him (probably because I was too nervous), but I was shocked that he happily engaged in discourse with me. His name was Chris, and he turned out to be very shy, nevertheless well-mannered, good-natured, and curious with a disarming decorum—a true southern gentleman. He lived in Alabama but had recently discovered the playground of Fort Lauderdale. He was getting a divorce (his sexuality was still a secret), and he had a twenty-one-year-old. Chris worked in a steel mill, and for the first time in his forty-plus years, he was starting to explore his latent desires.

There was a visceral sexual tension between us, but I was surprised to observe his body quiver like mine had out of nervous excitement when I had started sexually experimenting. We made our way into a private corner of the steam room, and with trepidation, Chris started to suck my dick. He told me that I was his first, which I didn't believe, but the way he handled it confirmed his claim. He caressed it like he didn't know what to do with it and then licked the head before getting the courage to put it in his mouth. I'm glad it was brief, because along with a lack of technique came scraping teeth. I couldn't believe it—he really was a novice. I felt flattered and honored, yet responsible for his first experience. I remembered the angst of my own first experiences and did my best to coach him through. I wanted it to be good and memorable for him, and what ruined it for me when I was exploring my sexuality was feeling obligated. So I firmly expressed a lack of judgment, embarrassment, and disappointment should he not want to do anything or feel uncomfortable at all.

I was shocked by how put together he was on the outside, yet so inexperienced in his sexuality. Chris was a reminder of my innocent and impressionable years. It's perplexing to fathom how many adult men (even married to women) repress their inclination toward physical expression with other men. For me, what I thought would be fun times became a responsibility when I realized their vulnerability—a responsibility to coach them about their own timing and self-respect. For Chris, I wanted to fast-forward him through all of his upcoming learning curves, to hold his hand and skip him over all of the bullshit, so that he wouldn't have to suffer the growing pains. I want for him and all alike a panacea—and I'm realizing now, especially after reading *A Return to Love* by Marianne Williamson, that *love is* the panacea.

ANNECY

I chuckled to myself as I let out random, muffled cheers—little bursts of joy as I strolled through the quaint town of Annecy, France. It was magical, even on a drizzly day: the Alps, the lake, the cobblestone alleys, and the colorful buildings—what a sight! I got a little choked up. I was overwhelmed with gratitude, at peace with myself, content with my life in general, and grateful to be alive, to be living my life with intent and self-command, coordinating my passion for languages with the fulfillment of another personal goal: finishing school.

On the train ride back to Grenoble, France, I was in awe at the beauty of the Alps, so majestic, our miniscule train hugging the side of the mountain, clinging onto the tracks, the snow like lace fringe, reflecting the midday sun. As we barreled off the mountain into a valley of rolling green hills, my excitement turned to tears, overcome as I was to witness the wonder.

I also had another epiphany: my life experiences had brought me to that moment. I had created a life on my own terms. I embrace the struggles and thank the lessons as gifts of earned wisdom and strength. I had discovered my individuality, and I will defend my autonomy at all costs! I had liberated myself! I had come so far, and in that moment I didn't want to be alone. I wanted to share the splendid bliss with Kirk. That train ride, with all its vicissitudes, was a metaphor for my life. The adventures, challenges, triumphs, and thrills of personal victories were all made sweeter by my being able to share them with Kirk. His nonjudgmental and unconditional love for me (especially when I didn't even love myself) and his understanding, acceptance, and validation of me have nurtured a positive force within, and I'll forever be grateful! I thank the universe for the opportunities to earn my self-conviction. I've never known such power, nor realized that I was capable all along.

Billy Ray was just an innocent boy from Idaho who loved to tumble. We had a lot to learn, my friend. I love you!

EPILOGUE

I wanted others to make me happy. Being the youngest of six in my family, I was accustomed to being rescued. However, on my own, the contradictory "help" that I got (validation through sex) was more damaging and fleeting than my justifications tried to deny. I wanted to believe the hype about sexual attraction being tantamount to social inclusion and personal acceptance.

Sex came too easily, and I used it as my coping mechanism and crutch. But it was only a temporary Band-Aid that left the wounds bare as the scabs ripped off with it. The orgasmic escape always ceased, and reality set in, like awakening from a dream before the good part but not being able to recreate it or pick up where it was so rudely and prematurely interrupted. I never addressed underlying issues, instead compounding them with guilt, shame, disrespect, and disappointment.

I seemed to attract other "damaged" people, as if we gravitated toward each other. Usually, how I felt about myself determined how low I'd go for my conquests. I exploited them. I used them like a drug to feed my insatiable need for validation and to placate my infinite insecurities. I was such a coward—too immature to face my own demons, always running, relocating, blaming. It's impossible to run from yourself, though. It sounds so elementary, but it took me many harrowing lessons to finally grasp this significant truth.

Even though I used men, didn't we use each other? Did they not take equal advantage of my compromised state and enjoy the virile pleasure of my body? I did my best not to lead anyone on—including myself. I wanted to change frequency—to evolve into a more dignified self. My role had to change. The universe has been gracious and generous with daily gifts of inspiration, people, conversation, experiences, etc.—reinforcing my gratitude for life.

I chased unmet needs. Instead of healing my core issues, I kept myself distracted by staying busy—my way of being there for myself when others weren't. However, I have gratitude for those special friends who were pivotal to my growth, helping me to avoid destructive pitfalls. They were monumental in helping me to discover and develop my own fortitude I didn't recognize inside. Gratitude is my source of abundance and peace of mind that can only come from within. I have a sense of empowerment from taking charge and transforming my personhood. I feel alive, and life feels almost transcendent. I'm hopeful. It keeps getting better and better—life is worth living, and I love it!

Home is that inner peace, that strength you can always rely on when life knocks you down. Now that I've learned some things, I want to share. I know that it is a power greater than myself that aligns the right people in my life at the right times and in the right places. By them believing in me and just loving me as I am, I'm set free. I feel compelled to contribute my empathy, my compassion, and my stories. If I can help liberate another soul, it will mean the world to me. Healing from my past is such a sweet release—to finally let it all go and just be me, present, loving, forgiving.

Giving up who I was in order to conform wasn't worth it. I didn't want to go through the discomfort, pain, and risks that accompany coming out, but eventually, I had to make a critical choice: I could either live for others' expectations and belong (which is no happy life) or have the courage to live an authentic life and embrace individuality (which is empowering). The paradox of believing in an institution that didn't believe in me was choosing to be a victim, and I grew to resent it. I regret wasting a lot of precious time, energy, emotion, and momentous life. There could be no more riding the fence.

I used to be consumed by anxiety and a sense of doom, expecting the worst from my family and society at large. The fear of a mediocre, lackluster existence motivated me to create my own interesting life story. I believe that we all seek a witness to our lives, validation of our worth and contribution, and assurance that we matter.

We all can choose to move on, to embrace the natural evolution, and to enjoy our journey. Even inaction is a choice. We can choose to improve our lots in life. I believe that striving for personal excellence will earn respect. I also believe that divine guidance will resonate with my life path.

I've traveled to many places trying to reclaim myself, overcoming obstacles, conquering fear and personal demons, and feeling lonely and ostracized. I've developed from a passive people-pleaser lacking self-esteem and -confidence into a mighty, independent force I've always wanted to claim as my own. From extremes to in between, I feel like I've already lived a fuller, more fulfilling life than I ever realized could be mine. I've learned not to underestimate myself or downplay the significance of my life. Self-discovery has been a continuous, invigorating progression. I'm not a refugee anymore. I'm a citizen of this world, and I proudly yet humbly reclaim my rightful place in it. I celebrate.

As Friedrich Wilhelm Nietzsche said, "I am who I must be!"

Made in United States
North Haven, CT
08 May 2023